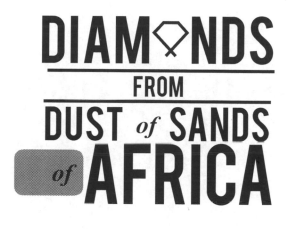

DIAM◇NDS
FROM
DUST *of* SANDS
of AFRICA

A BOOK OF ENLIGHTENING AND CONTEMPORARY POETRY

EDITED BY CHOENE ALLEY SEMENYA

CHOENE ALLEY SEMENYA   TSHEDISO SEROKI

PARTRIDGE

To order additional copies of this book, contact
Toll Free 800 101 2657 (Singapore)
Toll Free 1 800 81 7340 (Malaysia)
orders.singapore@partridgepublishing.com

www.partridgepublishing.com/singapore

BOOK DEDICATIONS

Dedications by Choene Alley Semenya:

For Caron,
To all my siblings (Jack, Jeff, Jonas, Mapule, Matlou and Tebogo)
To my mother, you have always been the best!

Dedications by Tshediso Seroki:
For my children,
To Jayson, Thabang and Johnson,
To my Mother, you watered me to grow to be the best out of me!

'It always seems impossible until it's done.'

Nelson Mandela

Acknowledgements

We would like to express our profuse gratitude to the many people who have been with us throughout the journey of writing this book; to all those who provided support, read, offered comments, allowed us to quote their remarks and assisted in the editing, proofreading and design. We would like to thank Partridge Publishing house, Singapore for granting us an opportunity to publish this book, the very first of our own.

I, **Choene Alley Semenya**, want to thank my girlfriend, my brother, Jack and my mother as well as the rest of my family and all my friends, who believed in me, supported and encouraged me in spite of all the time it took me away from them. Quite honestly, it was never an easy ride. Let me not forget to admit that I am greatly indebted to Ma'am Makhafola, my amazing high school English teacher, who made me fall so irresponsibly in love with literature and taught me as much the best of English language there could ever be. Above all, I would be ungrateful not to give special thanks to He who is in Heaven, The Almighty God, for the protection, strength and guidance He has granted me all these years.

I, **Tshediso Seroki**, would like to thank Jason Exquizit for the amazing mentorship, for helping me to unleash my full potential and recognizing my flairs; this significantly helped me build confidence in literature and to grow both as a person and as a writer. I would also love to acknowledge the support and magnitude of belief that my family had on me throughout my trials and tribulations; big ups to my kids for always enlightening me. Thanks to God, You are great all the time.

Finally yet importantly, we beg forgiveness of all those who have been with us over the course of the years and whose names we have failed to mention.

God bless you all.

Contents

PART I: SELECTED POETRY

PART II: AUTHORS' MUSE

PART I

SELECTED POETRY

HERE I LIVE

From grounds and sounds grounding my everlasting skin,
since seems to look like Sins of my skin.

Here I live.

Soil nourished by skeletons of fathers who went down the ground to seek
for gold –
Crowns of Kings and Queens forged from shattered men underground
while walls of their families crumble to the ground for Minimum wage.

Flesh mocks the empty stomach –
Prayers said to broken Monarch.

Here, life is for the dead when living die from empty promises.
Mother, I will grow to see your smiles blossoming like fresh Petals.
I have seen your magic touching my tears to giggles.

With face full of frowns you smile still holding prayer dear to your heart
like a Catholic nun;
To believe in God who starves His kids seems like a different Dream.

Here I live.

Your bosom rests my big head as lullabies swivel around my cranium.
Sleep is not for nights when shining armour covers
Skies when bodies Fall.

Guns keep shuttering life – distant lands, up in smoke,
Lungs burdened, heaving means last breath draws near.
Mother, behold me from Nimbus,
for this here is heavy on me like Golden Halo.

Behold me! Behold me!

Tshediso Seroki

THIRTEEN

I was born in Middle East in the outskirt of a state of Palestine –
Abducted at birth and my father executed when I was thirteen;
We buried him alone, bade him goodbye, in the midst of night.
Our desires and dreams, as family, put to fire and set alight.

Aware that our knight, the hope and the warmth with him are gone,
We felt unsafe, uncared for, deserted by life – with menace sworn.
I was only thirteen years old when I was targeted to be raped,
Brutal a man who wished to ravish and leave my womanhood reshaped.

I witnessed my mother ravished – my fear remains indissoluble till today,
Take it straight from me, I laid back, retreated, with hopeless anguish
obfuscating my way.
At only thirteen, O Lord, I saw how my mother endured the brutality of
wild man –
My heroine, violated at the expense of my well-being as best as one can.

Which despicable man lets a woman go through such torment,
While I, the innocent the child, my soul from within weeping tears of sad
lament?
Life in Middle East was never fair on us we absconded to a better state,
Travelled through a desert, to as farther as our feet could possibly take.

Life was hell –with a knife I was ready to stab into my troubled heart,
Bleed to death for as long as me and torture could live apart.
With a pistol I was ready to shoot right to the level of my head,
For my life was just of pain and unworthiness –I felt as good as dead.

Either death or dignity – we crossed the desert scared to live, scared to die;
For it seemed like only the stars were peaceably with us from the sky.
Just give to God what belongs to God, and to earth what belongs to earth;
Today it marks thirteen year since my father died, and as I sit and methinks –
I'm sadly reminded now of his untimely death.

Choene Semenya

Ravish: rape; **indissoluble**: unbreakable; **obfuscating**: puzzling, bewildering; **absconded**: ran away; **methinks**: I think

WHAT I WILL BRING

I won't bring you heaven to earth,
but I will learn to clothe your scars.
I won't lie and say I will go to the moon and back for you –
NO I won't, yet I will bring your fears to a halt.
I will neither challenge your independence
nor your decision yet
I will offer Perspective and Reason.

I will not say I will give you my heart on a silver platter,
yet I will keep you under my chest and lungs –
For I will learn to find breath with you and within you.
Smiles are priceless tokens,
yet the value of face full of light is
The greatest Price.

I Will bring you pleasure in friendship, for gems are rare to find.
I will safe keep your giggles every time you burst into a joyful trance.
And like Pandora's Box
I will keep your happier times intact to remind
You of Joy when Pain Visits.

I'm not a perfect man I'm far from it, yet I will clean my closet,
Bury skeletons to see you into passage of life without fear.
I will offer time when you don't have,
I will rip the heart off pendants that hold clocks hostage
so you can have all time in the world.

I will give you intimacy –
I will bring and make romance a fairy tale!

Tshediso Seroki

FROM *Unrequited Love*

I'll be there when you succumb to my love: to gloat, to see you weep;
I'll catch your tears on the flow,
Yes, I'll wipe off your cheeks below.
I'll be with you and you'll not have to see me limp or leap or creep.
I'll be waiting for you to touch me, to smile, perchance to pout your lips
and sigh –
I'll hold your back if you fall,
Yes, I'll lean you against the wall.
I'll be very quick to steal your kiss and yet screamingly sharpish to hold
you nigh.
I'll be there to soothe you, I'll even buy you a red rose;
I'll harken to your heartbeat,
Yes, I'll make you swear never to cheat.
I'll be awaiting you to blush when I peruse you prose;
I'll watch you relinquish and say: 'Oh Choene, you've won!'
Yes, I'll hear you admit you love me, and that we're on.

Choene Semenya

Unrequited: (of love) not returned by the person that you love; **succumb:**
give in; **gloat:** to show that you are happy about your own success or
somebody's failure; limp: **walk awkwardly; screamingly sharpish:**
extremely quick; **harken:** listen; **elsething:** something else; **peruse:** read;
relinquish: give up

3-TONE

Let me unzip my skin for you to find refuge in my wounds from which I
have bled,
Take my spine for pillow and rest your head to learn how many times
I have been breaking for holding into empty promises.

Convictions

When eyes close like doors, screams still on my palate like broken vinyl.
I can't hold on into lies for they have sketched empty mountains,
Rivers no longer know their flow, for stillness stir
The air in the direction of limping winds.

Declaration

Life measured with scars is more meaningful than face full of dying smiles,
This body, a coffin decorated with dead roses.
Nothing grows here, only remnants of broken skies.
Who deems life when we have died on our Knees?

Homophones

For what we knew
there is nothing new,

Beds nursing the sick
salvation in silent books we seek.

In this fight nothing if left
for they keep saying left.

We keep our war close to our broken souls
we are champions of haunted homes.

Tongue to lisp the lips when saliva boils,
for truth is a tool when reality uncoils.

Tshediso Seroki

DEEDS OF THE HUMANS

The slayer

Thoughts of the slayer throughout the day:
A thought to rob and a thought to slay.

A killer

There are two times that fulfill a killer's will:
With his mind and his soul both at ill,
It is a time to maraud and a time to kill.

Huntress

Never shall a reputable huntress fire her little gun,
Nor hunt dead all animals in the forest just for fun.
A good huntress never creeps or leaps or hunts in the rain;
It matters nought how wee, but she has nothing to gain –
So dear huntress, never creep or leap or hunt in the rain again.

The swain

He cannot woo; he dares not propose:
Neither can he consummate nor give a lady a rose.
Now his fatal attraction seems to be dying down,
And he dares not to let it out or let it drown.
O, what philtre shall succour he here be
If not reveal he his love to her and live free!

Choene Semenya

Slay: kill; **maraud**: search to attack, rob or kill; **consummate:** make something complete or perfect**; fatal attraction**: deep feelings of love; **philtre**: love portion; **succour**: help

LET ME MAKE A FAUX PAS

On barefoot upon thin shells
Time runs magic out of memory spells.
To err is Human

Beds made out of skeletons
We lie with our Dead past.
Haunted are pillows we put our heads to rest on.

Stomach welcomes poverty like warm embraces,
Hunger pangs angry faces.
Shadows cover empty spaces
Of falling temples,
Prayers await fainting church bells;
Men mastered their fates to wreck ships they command.

Tshediso Seroki

Make faux pas: fall, err

THE BEGINNING OF A NEW LOVE

O my cherished, never shall I get enough of your beauteous sight:
Unless perhaps, if you shall fulfill my wish to see you ev'rynight;
And cheer me up but with your hilarious tales to grow my sanity –
That shall I not break the faith of our durable wall for pride or for vanity!
Or surrender to a gob of temptations and infatuations which may constitute pain;
Or sing sorrowful songs and have my heart broken to smithereens yet again.
This is the beginning of a new love; after such daunting solitude, hopefully
I have all the vim in the world to live a life – though some say love is a bully,
Yet I still say that I love you with the special love that was made just for you and I –
Whether the wind blows warm or cold I'd persist to love you, but don't ask me why.
O dear, synchronise this love, let it live and show people how love is meant to be;
Kiss never any other lips than mine, or be muffled in the arms of any man other than me.
And let you, my sweet, the charade and the lust of day fade through the brightening air;
Hence that with the fidelity of a growing life, I too show that to love so much
is my flair.

Choene Semenya

Infatuation: an intense feeling of love that lasts for a short time; **daunting solitude**: intimidating loneliness; **vim**: energy; **predicate**: say, declare; **synchronicity**: the fact of two alike things happening at the same time; **charade**: pretense; **fidelity**: faithfulness; **flair**: talent

STATE OF AMNESIA

Where many forgot the Marshall Law colouring streets red,
Yellow mellows ridding dusty roads
Like angry horse Men.
Gun shots, another body adds to statistics
'Tis a black child who died.

At what expense must promising heroes keep dying before their time?
Sons were forced to exile their homelands in search for freedom;
how we forgot the essence of brotherhood when love is no longer fought for.

There is romance where lovers write letters to their beloved from foreign
lands,
Now freedom has fallen into wrong hands.
Sons now go by
Night and at the breaking of dawn they return home inebriated –
Mothers on their knees have been a lifetime struggle yet we forgot.
Lovers buried Lovers
Mothers buried Fathers,
Now homes are falling

Lovers now bury each other under
Battle grounds Where accusations are the seed.
Now Mothers Kill fathers to inherit
Insurance payouts.
We forgot family values . . .

In case you forgot what freedom stands for,
breathe,close your eyes and see how KALUSHI'S neck tied a knot with
death.
Hear door of his loving heart
crumbling as his body danced to unseen tune.
Deep in the sea of stars, he gave up his life for us to see our way.

Morality acts, lost like Unwanted habits
We have forgotten how to sing ourselves to life;

Magic of elders recognise us no longer,
for we have abandoned our old ways
to find solace in foreign gods.

See, where I stand the sun is clear
Intention is fair.
Taught ways of survival in the jungle only to
die on concrete forest;

We forgot.

Tshediso Seroki

Amnesia: Loss of memory; **Yellow Mellows**: Big Police vans in the time of apartheid they were called hippos; **KALUSHI**: a name of young Freedom fighter whose full name is Solomon KALUSHI Mahlangu

UNTITLED

Tin man holds empty heart for a Temple, broken knees for Prayers.
Nothing Grows Here except Nothing.

Tshediso Seroki

DEAR OLD SHE!

Dear old she! –
The sun is tanning and battering
Her skin,
Greying her hair, fading her beauty;
She's gone frail!
Youth has fled her, and hence decrepitude
has befriended her –
For never the twain shall meet.
But still she rises in the dawn,
And she sweeps and she mobs and she cooks;
Without wee help to ease her daily chores.
Her days go over with fatigue in her body,
But she never whines!
And to add, at night she sleeps but with one eye –
Stretching her ears,
and not moving lest she misses falls of feet,
Of some naughty brutal man who may want to
break into her house, and ravish her.
It's like in a forest,
With only herself to hear breathe;
And to hear sigh –
Her eyes fixed on the scrambling curtain
of a broken window,
Feeling the cold of a frigid wind
that blew the trees
To rustle with a noise burdened with guilt.
Agitatedly peeking at her locked door
Biting her tongue in the loneliness of her blues
and her qualms;
Her threadbare blanket blows dust and
makes her sneeze, and expectorate – ail!
Lightest things of her belongings blown away
from her ragged stands and whacks on the floor;
O dear old she! Never does she rest,
Because whenever she learns to slumber

Is already dawn —and has she to wake up
And accomplish her daily chores, again.

Choene Semenya

Decrepitude: state of being old and in poor health; **brutal**: cruel; **ravish**: rape, violate

DISTANCE

Wrists give pulse a beauty of life when all seem out of reach –
Roses know palm prints of the sun at
Every breaking dawn.

Flaws are lessons like wilting petals;
Every flower has a story either of love or War.
Some stories are conceived when battles
roar even stones can build great walls.
Emotions sometimes understand miracles yet hearts still
wants to calculate distance between beats at every rhythm.
Infinity is when spirit jumps to rejoice love.

Tshediso Seroki

WHEN DID I GROW SO JEALOUS?

When did I grow so jealous, from where comes this aberration?
I've become someone almost impossible with pride,
I've grown so much hateful it exceeds my height –
Jealousy, does it come with love or does it come with obsession?
What feeling is this so cumbersome to a mortal breathing kind?
What contempt? What hate so pure it renders me savage?
What if I admit that I love her and use that as leverage,
But what reflection shall I get? What shall it impart to my mind?
A foolhardy verdict that may not build me, nor may it break me –
Nor shall it suffice me, nor fill my heart with utmost pleasure,
But notions of impropriety which shall torment me to all measure.
Aye, I love this lady! – Nay, I love her not, hence if love then be
a genuine sentiment so gently mused to the coffers of my heart
True as truth and fine fair; when shall this resentment in me but depart?

Choene Semenya

Aberration: oddness, abnormality; **cumbersome**: very heavy; **savage**: brutal, violent; **impropriety**: rudeness

WAR CHILDREN

First time I saw a genuine smile was a war torn area on a photograph;
I didn't want to look at amputated arms, legs stumps and
The story that draped their pain.

I see body parts for headlines, orphans who pose with guns in their hands;
Maybe something is mysterious about children walking over landmines –
Days of their youth flashing before their eyes.
'Tis war, nobody cares if children live or die.

I have seen grounds with blood of the innocent in Aleppo,
Christmas carols for sounds of bombs that resembles Breaking Hearts.
A mother shouts Allah in hope for the safe return of a child
sent for bread and milk.
Every crumbling wall exposes the naked truth where
bodies lie naked and lifeless.

A child in Burundi still dreams to fly paper kites in the strangest of them
winds, he saw how rebels ripped his village apart,
There, lamentably, he sits, and hopes for sleep to bring better days.
Love letters never reached lovers, for the messenger was shot en route.
Bring back our girls! a slogan for missing girls in Nigeria,
Boko Haram a nightmare to young mothers
and promising daughters.

To this day Santa knows not of gift of life missing in Middle East,
Bodies of dead villages in Forests of Uganda.
Santa knows more of Snow and Chimneys, snowman and Christmas trees,
Not dust falling from demolished building and streets where blood stains
mark where Heroes died.

War children,
I have seen how your innocence has been taken from you –
How you wished for play grounds not graveyards.
War children,
I have seen your knees for grace, how your face collected frowns for memories. I still wish to undo what is done.
Orphans often blame God and Allah for their loss, even the man on the cross.

One day your face will smile, and clouds will not be full of smoke and toxic fumes, only air full of life.
War child live, I know your scars are deeper and the sepsis still hold onto the pain.
Live.

Tshediso Seroki

1,2,3 LOVE IS IN THE AIR

1.

The air is dense with particles of our inhalations,
ONE lung for the breath of TWO;
ONE heart for two beats;
We are ARITHMETIC.

2.

TWO eyes for ONE vision,
TWO arms for ONE warm embrace,
Cover my scars with your Skin –
Keep me in under the red of Plethora....

3.

In the name of the sun, the wind and the pouring rain;
Your face like white of beautiful picked cotton holds my wishes,
My fingertips still hurt as your past pricked my prints
In search of your Smiles.
My heart changes it's palpitations at your very existence:
It Stops . . . starts . . . and stops again.
My sweat glands bursting
To precipitates of my Fear.
Love Triangles Brought me to my knees
In pursuit of You.

Tshediso Seroki

Arithmetic: Part of mathematics dealing with Manipulation and properties of numbers; **Plethora:** Excess bodily fluids particularly blood; **precipitates**-: the remains after a reaction.

MY FIRST TRUE LOVE

To Caron

O loveliest is my first true love
    and docile.
And honest in unconditional love
    and fine,
as fair as the scent of roses of spring,
do attract the bees in daylight once sprung red.
    And deep across pretentious love, lust and lies,
    midst a pool of broken hearts,
    and a profusion of infatuations,
Her true love is inspiring
    like a promising wish.

O song gleeful sung by gay birds
    in the morn of sun shining
bright and warm, like a love poem of a poet
    whose dedication is to his paramour.
Amidst all spurious-proven love in the face of the sky,
a dinkum feeling of love subsists only within her and I –
    Across the breadth and length of life
She shows me pure love – O dear Caron, I'm so shy;
    For in each day love's but growing old
Yet in her song it quickly shines bold.
    She tells me as humble her secrets
and trusts me most benign and most bounteous.

O crap! Who said Venda women are not beautiful?
    I mean look at her, just look at her –
She looks absolutely pulchritudinous –
Where have I travelled to see such beauty,
to Venda, perhaps?
My first true love, my muse, breathtaking –
Her smile, as humble as the tears of a fly;
    And her tangy lips, succulent and divine

And fine as she partakes of her fancy wine –
And her eyes appear so clear, like the face of a mountain pool –
O but her body what slender?
        Her body what foxy it makes me drool!
Her voice so sweet when she sings,
it makes me imagine lotsa things;
        She's absolutely ravishing and beautiful, O my!
I charm her with my words, staring her in the face;
        with her brown beautiful eyes sweeping all across me,
So much merriment fills in me I forget breathing is free
– O my first true love,
I am devastatingly besotted with her;
        O my true love,
        Is but hoped to be my last and only true lover.

Choene Semenya

Gleeful: thrilling, happy, exciting; **gay**: cheerful, lively; **paramour**: lover; **spurious-proven**: proven false; **dinkum**: true, sincere; **subsists**: exists; **bounteous**: generous; **devastatingly besotted**: extremely love-sick, too much in love

UNAGING LOVE

I saw forever on the white of your eyes,
Your words wired life to my skin where pigments lies.
The fibers of your hair my silk cotton,
You clothe my emptiness with your embraces,
No matter life toughest phases.

Oh! Humble servant of undying dreams,
Decibel levels of sanity brushed through the
frequencies of your palms.
Reason for breathing has come in your beauty.

The aisle you sauntered became garden of dreams
and every petal that touched the ground gave birth to an angel.
The safeguard of my faltering hope the fortress of wisdom;
Promises made under the sun –
When my heart skipped a beat,
To beat my thoughts in marathon for your love,
You promised me heaven under our radiant skin,
That you will stand by me till our skin
Wrap away our days,

You said you will find me attractive always,
even if the grey of my eyes cannot remember you.
You words still hold meaning when we have transformed to moving
earthquakes,
When my eyes lost sight you vowed to be my candle to lead my light.
I know you have taught my chest to breath in fashion of spinning windmills,
every breath drawn is you filling my lungs with life.

Our wrinkles now dance to the movement of our brittle bones,
everything we try – a stance of catching memories
through our filled hourglass.
On our window pane memory reminds us of our youth that has passed.

If my eyes be the mirrors to my soul then you are the reflection undefined,
When we forget our anniversary I promise to go outside and ask the stars
as their shine kept secrets of our nights sneak outs.
I wrote journals in forms of shooting stars.

Happily ever after is a place beneath your skin
where my existence is held dear like
a Holy Grail.

Tshediso Seroki

Sauntered: walked in a slow, relaxed manner

AT UNIVERSITY RES

For the lady who resides at 3rd floor

I meditate as I close my eyes, so much of her ravishing face,
The loveliest aesthetic art that brings me joy and grace –
The dimples in her cheeks, her small black eyes, her ethereally crafted lips;
If she were a waitress I'm confident her pocket would be flooding with tips.
O, beautiful is she, if I that may say. She is like a flower that never fades;
She's transparent, like a lake – her teeth pure white, shiny as new knife blades.
I infer, she is adorable when she sleeps and at dawn when she does awake,
Her kindness and her serenity, they mesmerize me –yup it's true, I don't fake.
And as for her hips, both voluptuous and curvilinear, like Mount Everest,
It would possibly take me months to climb to its Highest–
And by my lips, I swear, if she offers me a chance to kiss,
If that happenstance ever presents itself I'd definitely not miss.
The truth is simple, she appeases me and I so ample wish she would be mine;
But she frightens me –nevertheless, soon I'd dare her out on a date to dine.

Choene Semenya

Serenity: peaccfulness, calmness; **voluptuous**: having big seductive curves; **humongous**: huge; **happenstance**: luck; **ample**: much; **dare**: challenge, **ethereally**: seeming extremely delicate

DOORS

When one closes one Opens,
balance of things always throw faint hearted of their feet.
Some changed locks and keys to master
The art of opening secret passages to the Unseen.
Many doors to choose from,
yet One Leads to Destiny designated.

From rusty hinges of relationship door
we keep knocking until knuckles bleed,
no one wants to enter Gates of Hell.
Some doors lead to darkness,
Some to eternal light,
Some doors are caskets holding skeletons intact,
In fact some doors are Open graves.

We dance, cheer, drink our souls to movement of steady earth;
We take turns looking and seeking.
Some doors are stairways to peace,
Some doors are open for war to break,
Some doors are our father's fears
Others our mother's scars Inflicted.

Clouds are classic songs we dance for,
at times To Dead Beats.
We look forward even when we are gullible to circumstances.
See these doors are like deck of cards
Waiting to call the highest bid.
Our Doors are made from Glass and steel,
Taught that every door comes
With how to feel.

When another door closes the other one is a reminder
of The previous.

Tshediso Seroki

SOUGHT LOVE

How is it but for my part, such as I are,
When the energy I use to love thee is wasted –
Even though but for love alone
I come by wish, to proffer and to reciprocate;
Yet but thee, dost thou not love by the moon,
Dost thou not love freely, to fulfill my means;

O dear, O dear!
How on earth had I fallen in love with you,
For my wooing seems futile as I impart my love to you.
I am a loving gentleman, but true love upon thee stays misused.
If, in the breaking of day shall I perchance thy love receive
I would be thrice, three times happiest in this –
As skeptical whether all I perceive be deception or true;
Since all this fortune, thrice-fairest lady, comes to you.
Is pure luck if I may tell, to be loved so true to seek no new.

I fall for you, and yet, dear lady,
Doth thine love deny to honour my unfurnished state.
The magnificent, the fairest, the kindest love I possess worn with misery;
I might be bless'd with errors of courtship and so, I know,
But yet my heart thumps hence as not false –
Which rather therein works a miraculous magic in nature;
To adore thee so dearly, so graciously and fortuitously in excess.
O but you glamorous lady, be fair, be moderate, succumb thy love;
Thou art not too old to learn –in sum to aught and all,
Hence thou canst always learn to love me – to hold me and to cuddle me.

Let not but in my heart to fall for thee be a torment but delight,
In mine mind to meditate of thee be not bewildering but fulfilling,
And in mine soul to care for thee be not cumbersome, but light.
Myself, and all what is owned by I – in heart, in soul and in mind is thine;

I cannot give them away, nor can I lose or part from them,
Until sought, accepted, honouréd, requited by you.

Choene Semenya

To proffer and to reciprocate: to give and to receive; **skeptical**: doubtful; **deception**: dishonesty; **thrice-fairest**: wonderfully beautiful; **unfurnished state**: state of having no partner, being lonely; **fortuitously in excess**: by chance so much (to love her); **aught**: anything; **torment**: annoyance, irritation, punishment; **cumbersome**: very heavy, uneasy; **requited**: returned

IN A DECAYING SOCIETY

Sons rot in jail for facing crimes of their youth,
and society believes it's OK for young boys to know coldness of steel.
Freedom is like a metallic taste on the tongue after years of Imprisonment.

Communities breed empty households,
Where mothers wear garments of men and wear their shoes.
See, black communities are under attack,
Shebeens and taverns are hot spots when schools run empty lessons;
believe it or not our black homes blacker,
the darker the berry the sweeter the taste?

Not in black society.

Here mothers look at skeletons of their dying children,
like melting winter frost bites on lips of summer heat.
Everyone looks away when a young girl falls pregnant and shames
The Mother for what her daughter has done
See, innocence has lost its way in black communities.

Tshediso Seroki

A LETTER FROM A
REJECTED YOUNG MAN

Love you so bad to flirt,
Cuts so deep it hurts –
June is my month of birth,
Be with me for all its worth.
02 June 2014

Dear Yvonne

I never had love so bottomless and so great, so courteous, tremendous, and so certified. I pray you, though, that the love may not exceed as far-flung as to thus to woe me as you deny it to deny me –
To have the outstanding and forfeit of my humour. Tell me, O erratic lady; how far have you thought of me? Because I have thought of you through deep into the night to the breaking of a new dawn;
As I am ambitious in my wish –to pertain the desideratum I need. Oh, I have to fight for what I rigorously want, for I do oppose to grieve with quietude of a smitten heart. Stand as I am, I behold upon your visage the glorious lips that are fabricated but for my obdurate kiss –
Hence that my lips, be made as soft as yours, as fair can they be yours, yet I declare upon you but loss;
As you dismiss my love from the palate of your thoughts –
I have a fear you might envy or miss me when I'm gone. My patience is not so patient anymore, but fury in me is an illicit course, in law of my religion –
What emotion so contaminated and so rebarbative, but being issued with an imperishable love that suffices you, negates the hate and the anger.
'Tis dearly fated, you are mine, and I shall have you:
You shall not pity me, but you shall dote upon me.
But lest you refute me till doomsday, I shan't stay forever in waiting;
I the boy who is incapable of hate or anger –
Yet my handsome face shall scan reminiscently in your mind, and the power of my gracious voice will monitor your ears –

You will remember me when I'se moved forth;
From how I madly fell in love with you,
To how I sadly learnt to stop loving you.

Sincerely yours,
Gift

Choene Semenya

Certified: promised; **outstanding and forfeit of my humour**: to be owed
so much that I even lose my humour; **desideratum**: something strongly
needed or wanted; **obdurate**: firm; **you dismiss . . .of your thoughts**:
you decide not to think of my love anymore; **rebarbative**: disgusting,
unpleasant; **imperishable**: endless, never dying; **suffice**: satisfy; **negates**:
nullifies, denies, forbids; **lest you refute me till doomsday**: in case you
deny me for a very long time, **I'se**: similarly used I have

I WANT TO LIFE NOW

Mouths of our Oracles have been poisoned by rituals of myth.
Now is a past tense to a Promising life.
Forced to abandon the happy
To reside inside the Sad.

Look how heavy is your face.
Winter a place next to hell,
Nothing promises life here.

Every wise ear fall on deaf ear;
The empty is a place around our lips
The broken is our hearts and relationships.
The covenant is broken brothers in the Hood,
the culture nurtured from poverty and disease.
DEATH awaits the ghetto.

Faith is for the sad, hope for the dead;
Prayers for cracked mothers when daughters
trade body parts for airtime.

I want to Life Now.
I have been living yet don't know how –
Nothingness a place where mystery uncoils.
Shells are for weakened bodies,
Education for institutions,
Graduates for Statistics.

I want to Life Now.
The present opens door to let life flash in front of dead visions.
Dreams are for pillows,
ghettos are place for our Sorrows.
I want to Life out of my skin Color.
Black – a place where sick infants are sent to die

Rivers are worn out like skin perfected with drought.
Shacks know no power cables especially when lights Out.
The mystery of fire knows the flame when primus stove starts the fire,
One flame devours the whole community by night and spit out the remains
when morning comes like premature ejaculation.
Headlines about the poor,
Racism is not a disease so no cure.
Hi Ms. Zille,
I greet your colonialism with hand of miners who died in Marikana.

I want to Life Now.
I tricked death to keep breathing with lung full of bullet holes.
I magic the life my throat.
Adams for an apple bite,
men endangered species that's up for a fight?

I'm tired of doing the dying –
Where bodies are heavy, skins are weary,
Tongues cut, knees hammered,
I'm tired of doing the running away from Racism.
I'm tired of doing the burying.
I'm tired of the Anger, the frustration.
Suicide for the depressed,
Neck and ties for the compressed,
Tuxedos building pressure,
Anger snap shots for debt repayment.

I'm tired of the slavery.
I want to Life Now.
I don't want to do the I'm fine
Because I'm not.

I want to Life.

Tshediso Seroki

A FEELING THAT NEVER GAVE ME PEACE

Per night and day, each dawn a feeling came with the rise of sun,
a feeling devoid of truth and faith, but oddly full of treacherous fun –
That feeling was formidable, almost insurmountable, felt real and strong;
it truly touched deeply my heart, like the lyrics of Dolly Parton's song.
Almost, I succumbed, and a hopeless hope interlaced my heart, again;
presenting with manifestations of greed and reflections of pain.
Peace till eternity unknown, hate blazing within it like bonfire at night,
from this feeling that never gave me peace but always stole my delight.
Mercy not shown to the anxieties I had felt and endured within my fears;
The chronicles of my sad love stories, like blurred vision, unseen from my
tears –
It felt so fine, but with dire a deep vein hatred, like pure gold, I almost
acted blind
Because that feeling disarms even a divinely charismatic man off his
celibate mind;
A feeling of hateful love that invaded my heart, a sentiment of absolute
imperfection
which offered me peace never but evermore, till yesterday, showered me
with dejection.

Choene Semenya

Treacherous: capable of betraying; **formidable**: terrible, very deep;
insurmountable: overwhelming; **interlaced**: linked together; **divinely
charismatic**: holy and worshipping enthusiastically; **imperfection**: a state
of being not perfect; **dejection**: misery, unhappiness

MESSENGER FROM THE EAST

His word rose behind crumbling Mountains,
his voice coding beauty of flowing Fountains;
Palms moving with pouring rain
Body movements making waves to
Decorate contours on sands of Time.

Mother, let your children follow
The dancing winds, dismember your compass;
Around their smiles install beautiful rainbows.

Father, your lessons are learnt from the burning incense,
Behold your sons sinking their palms shaping barks from promising trees.
At every flow of every river lies
a mystery between the living and the dead,

Elders keeping taboos at bay for time
gives so much to say.
Cowhides on the ground seeking answers
Like alladin in clouds with his flying mat.

In Cosmos there are stars weeping
And wisdom in scars bleeding,
Shallow wormholes keep the belly
as immense as the Sea – swallowing seamen in search,
For mystery where the deep rest it's Beasts.
The telescopes beyond sight in quest for beauty out of reach.
Speech a mystery unrecognised when body movements rewrite Intent.

Villages in the far lands of imagination still beat
the drum to usher ancestral pulse in the coded air.
Children gather bare chested as elders clear throats for the yet to be told
stories. Valleys were once tears of angels,
Every ripple a new page opened for those who want to learn to dip their
dried skins.
Warriors still cover their faces and bodies with clan marks,

Mountain tops not to rest the white of snows but teach
young boys ways of Manhood.
These are old ways wrinkles of dying elder for wisdom of sages,
every layer as cold yet another new page life lives here.

Taboos hiding beneath tattoos,
Maidens covering their bodies with ancient stories of rivers that forever
flow;
Heads holding calabashes of respect,
incense to evoke spirits of chanting songstress.
Stars come down as bonfire holds flames.
Rain makers know shapes of moving clouds,
deciphering movement of colony of ants towards the
Anthill is second nature to those who holds dear ancient ways.

Child books sometimes hide meaning of wisdom you seek,
Learn patience from elders that speak.
For toothless mouth is open wide like Pearly Gates of heaven.
Behold your mouth for it's about to rain when dark clouds gather.

Tshediso Seroki

Incense: Substance burnt to release a fragrance especially for religious
or ancestral ceremonies; **Telescopes**: Instrument designed to make far
objects appear nearer. **Ripple**: Series of waves in water caused by an object
dropped in it.

TILL ETERNITY

I love you. Always have. Always will.
And I do not want months with you.
I want Years.
I want Eternity.
I want FOREVER.

Choene Semenya

WE WERE TAUGHT TO DIE

Umbilical cords for Strings of death when pulled from ghetto alleys
pushing Hustle it doesn't care if it hurts or painful,
Submit to cuffs and serve dead sun god;
The chalkboards still holds the white dye of the breaking bones while
running from stray bullets.
We were taught to dye the grounds with the red of our blood when we die.

Sticks and stones, young soldiers and terrifying war zones,
To have and to hold guns for a living
life in the slums has no meaning.

Ambulance and police lights to come between gang fights,
Reasons to open Fire unknown
in the deep of the ghetto there's no growth.

We were taught to dye streams with tears of unemployment,
When hope dies leaving behind disappointment.

Tshediso Seroki

WHEN TO THE ETERNITY

When to the eternity of love embraced in heart
With no particular sense of hate flickering past
The eyes that saw those whom I admired depart,
I evoke up the sorrowful memories I forgot at last;
I smile to many a thought of what from them I learnt –
And with old wounds and old woes now vanished,
I sigh the sigh of relief in that I know what they meant:
The impediments I endured proved love finished
From the hearts that had no hesitation to lie
For ill-advised and wrong doings at guilty sight,
And so their sweet lips and beauty disfigured to my eye;
Then can I love yet with sincere love, growing day & night, –
       The lady who loves me with love unencumbered,
       Whose lips are still pure, with no lies remembered.

Choene Semenya

Woes: many things leading to grief many sorrows; **impediments**: obstacles;
ill-advised: stupid; **disfigured**: spoiled, flawed; **unencumbered**:
unburdened

DAYS OF OUR YOUTH

Memory aches as we walk down the streets that once bled,
lungs full of bullet holes.
Breathe, they Said.

Kill them young, with guns, drugs and violent crimes.
Let them smoke their lungs in their times.
Stones turned out of heavy smokers, when dreams die
In the ghetto nobody wants to get Involved.

Razor blades to cut through the wrist to cease painful times,
fashion trends dropping morals like low standards of dialect missed by
Youth; Fresh graves awaits palm prints of tiny feet that
Walks through open thighs to the Dustbins.
Morality questioned by rate of Mortality,
Who dies when days are still young,
Us the discarded youth failing family trees.

Forced to do time behind walls of our ignorance,
We have marks as chains holding on to what dreams can never be.
Grave yards pay homage to young dead bodies.
Nobody looks when young minds drown in rivers of alcohol;
We render epiphanies as they lose the wealth of their Youth.

Taught to remain redundant when everyone lives expectations,
Taught to fight but not given a reason to fight –
We lament with prayers of our broken mothers,
after all we are their Sons and daughters.

Tshediso Seroki

THE ILL YOUNG WOMAN'S ELEGY

For Mokgadi Lorraine Mabote

In memoriam her late friend

There lies a young woman who critically and suddenly fell ill.
She'd lain listless abed; her body succumbed to an ailment still.
Her final words on earth were: 'Dearest pal, now I'm ascending
For where hate ain't exist, nor prejudice, nor condescending –
Yet I'll tell you one thing, pal, I'll miss overmuch all our studies;
And I'll be very cold not to mention that we were great buddies.
I, in the singular, know that my quietus will bring you heartache forever,
But the Elysian cherubs will take a particular care of me; mourn for me never.
Though, too, the whole shebang there, is precise to my desires;
For where there ain't hate, there's no extinguishing of fires –
Hence, I'd be dejected to see you relinquish life in your boundless sorrow.
In fact, posthumously, study further hard; study as if there ain't the morrow
–Sombre, are I, too, that I shall anon breath my last;
This is a consummation our palship led; oh blast!'

Choene Semenya

In memoriam: from Latin meaning in memory of; **quietus**: death; **Elysian cherubs**: heavenly angel; **boundless sorrow**: endless sadness; **sombre**: very sad; **anon**: soon; **palship**: friendship; **posthumously**: happening after someone's death

STAIRWAYS TO THE GHETTO

We have been jumping stages like Super Mario.
Our stories start with sad Endings.
The wave of acceptance keeps rising and at every fall,
we fall apart in pursuit of Fitting In.

Coffins have been fitting our bodies like suites;
We're only fit to die and grave yards to bury us like Secrets.
We have been mimicking our fallen heroes and
adopting their doctrines that we have to
die to see freedom.

Fathers used to be role models, now they are models without roles – useless.
Mothers of broken sons, songstress to sing their broken hearts to sleep;
It's our acts of lullaby songs when we sleep into the forced Night.
Being told to fight yet never given a reason to fight.

We keep missing chapters in our lives, from being infants to children
soldiers. Wars have been making their make on walls of our crumbling
innocence.
When father brings up his right fist is not a freedom gesture but
Act of his marital vows till death do us Part,
Our mothers die, as they bleed to death yet keeping their
Hearts opened for change.

We have been jumping stages of our youth to become young irresponsible
fathers, who chill with boys for soccer games and late night drinking
sessions. We coach each other from inexperienced tongues. Nobody taught
us responsibility for many of us grew up with absent fathers.

See in cacophony of screams it's our sisters who are forced to womanhood
in the Hood, alleys groom monsters for shadows still hold spirits of sons
who never went back home. Father, we have been dying:
from silence to violence it's us who sing
When we descend.

We pilot pain for we are the ones chosen to fly paper kites in the pouring Rain. Abortion clinics, it's my sisters who queue to turn wombs into tombs. Spirits of aborted infants never die but haunt the body.

Tshediso Seroki

LOVE

Love! real founder of most heartaches thou art!
Which torments my heart and soul and mind;
Wherefore hast thou invaded my contented heart
If thus thine intents were not serene and kind?
How must I have held thee? Or kept thee fine
From battering winds and discontent too,
When in disguise thou didst seekest joy of mine
To tear it wholly asunder and shove it through
The gates of consummation and aflame in hell,
Hast thou not sought peace at first and joy?
Perchance if not a haven then a place to dwell,
To let the summer sun shine, harmless and coy,
Hast thou not vowed to keep Boitumelo with me,
And let her love even in tedium and moods sweet be?

Choene Semenya

Serene: calm; **wholly asunder**: completely apart; **consummation**: termination; **coy**: modest

THE COLOR OF MY SINS

Church!
A place to seek refuge and hope to the hopeless,
Temple of God decorated with sinister sins of dying fathers, orphans and
discarded off-springs.

I have been trying to fit in my skeleton,
yet my sins are overweight and crashing my spine.
Please don't colour my sins black,
I have been black enough even shadow of death
Looks like light at the end of the tunnel.

Please don't colour my sins red, for red is the color of danger
I have seen taking form when streets were no longer safe haven
for young children and promising black boys and girls,
see red is the target mark behind our hoodies in our neighbourhood.
We get shot because we have inherited the stories of our forefathers
Who died trying to skin off their Sins.
Target practice to shoot the innocent for their red blood nourishes
pavements with screams of dead dreams.

Please don't colour my sins green,
for I have seen greener postures nourished by flesh of fallen heroes.
See every wave of color holds a story and my sins take form every time
I breathe.
Green bar coded ID left the smell of scorn as I stand on the line for a dream
of rainbow nation to take form.

Tshediso Seroki

Sinister: menacing, nasty; **discarded:** rejected; **nourished:** feed, cared for

GONE WITH LOVE

Gone, and gone with love!
Up forlornly went my breath
Down my body sank, of death
I but recall, in love with you intensely how I fell
And evermore was I there while you were unwell
I broke jokes to you to keep you calm
And I took care of you when you broke your arm
I waited for you to admit that you loved me
And to assure me that we would soon together be
I waited for you to discard your pride and take part
But I doubted that your love resided in a confused heart
And so long I cared for you till my love did decay
As I loved you in vain till the sun came and took me away!
Pity when I was gone I learnt that you loved me too
And that it was belated of time that I could then be with you
Because now I'm gone, and with true love I'm gone!

Choene Semenya

VICTORIA FALLS

Her pulse resembles her beat everytime she cries;
she keeps her flow wrapped in stories untold –
Truth in her purity the only melody unfold.

She keeps her feet rooted to the ground everytime her
Face is smashed against the rocks;
She keeps breaking into surfaces of her unsung songs.
Rhythm of sadness keeps reminding her why she keeps falling,
Victoria Falls for no reason when anger meets alcohol as weekend waters
Break like ancient calabashes.
She falls with her arms stretched to the sky,
with no help to nurse her wounds.

Time takes turns to find tunes synchronised with Victoria's Rhythms,
She watched the sands of time as they stopped her bleeding soul,
indeed time heals.
She mastered the art of crying until her tears turned to violin string across
her cheeks – see, every tear creates music, she dances.
From her beauty sleep under the full moon she wakes her inner broken
pieces
To be one with flow of life,
Like tides imprinting their new rise on shores, she rises.

Her fall no longer hurts as she mastered the alchemy of turning sadness
to joy.
Victoria forever flows like her falls ingested rainbows
To carry the white of her flow
like white of snow.

She fell in love with a rock hoping to break it into Cornerstone,
yet she keeps breaking, it doesn't hurt anymore as
She dances herself back to Life.

Tshediso Seroki

Calabashes: ground gourd, in African Tribes It's used during ritual gatherings; **Imprinting:** symbolise. **Cornerstone:** vital element

MIRAGE

How jejune is a wish per se when it remains but just a mirage,
Lest for love alone my heart desires without adventure and courage?
How dull can a wish be if it has no intentions of being achieved,
And let my soul rather rejoice with mirth instead of being grieved –
'Twixt honesty and truth, of which shall I at least be true to myself?
For not in love neither, shall I denounce my fear and succumb to love itself;
What do I do now that I know not what to do? It confounds me –
If Kafkaesque fears had not precluded me but stood still and let nature be,
I would not fail my wish, as much as it would fail me not;
That therefore from love I shall harvest peace, and remember not
The worst that broke me and the secrets contained in my amber glass.
O, in advancing quest of my utmost, love trial has reached an impasse –
Because I are to secure a lover whose love is of truth and not of pity,
A lady whom shall give me no reason whatsoever of insecurity.

Choene Semenya

Jejune: dull, boring; **mirth**: merriment, fun & humour; **denounce**:
disown; **confounds**: confuses; **Kafkaesque**: terrible, horrible; **impasse**:
end, termination

EMEKA

I'm a man and a man is filth,
i have been in my skin long enough my skeleton can't remember me.
The anchors in my soul shattered in more than one place.

Emeka

Pendulums proving arms parallel to the sky, its grace I'm so much hoping
for –Tears on your face, my kryptonite; it's sad to walk around with a heavy
heart, chest keeping air just to live on by.
Emeka, breathing regrets is like sniffing toxic fumes killing the mind . . .
Emeka I'm a Man.

These ink carvings hide my scars,
at every blink of an eye i wish to see slow motion of my flashing life.
Emeka, I embedded seeds in my soul to bury my insecurities;
Yet my sanity escapes my scalp every time I scratch my skull for answers.

Emeka I'm a man.

Tshediso Seroki

Emeka: An Inbox name meaning God has done so much

AN INFAMOUS FEELING

For Webster Selolo, a dear friend!

By the time he partook of his love with bliss,
Still more love-struck had he without her kiss –
But patiently, he bore, as ever was he fain
To love infinitely; albeit was he driven insane
By her habit that evermore disfigured her attitude –
When she left his heart unattended, and solitude,
A massive pain, devoured his passion and torn him apart,
And evicted an infamous feeling of love from his heart.
But as of right, he vowed to love her to his soul's end,
In fact, some there be not so much of her could he fend;
He had a feeling so concise, unambiguous and tangible –
Though his love and his fear were growing incompatible.
So be gone! be gone! be gone the feeling he'd cut his skin;
Lastly, if not unfortunately, he died slowly from within!

Choene Semenya

Partook: shared; **fain**: prepared; **disfigured**: flawed, spoiled; **fend**: resist;
solitude: loneliness

I COLLECT ANTIQUES

I collect antiques from my grandmother's old room divider,
I never touched her dark brown little puppies made out of ceramic
until I saw them collecting dust like an old boulders.
Her brass vases for stars the house still shines bright
in her memory.

Her floral table cloth, baby pink as I remember it;
She had her wedding photo on the white painted walls,
Black and white my great grandfather dressed in black a suit;
My grandma's beauty embraced her youth, her bracelet complimenting
her white nuptial gown.

Her old record player collected all her words bringing life to us her
Grandchildren, together as we dance to her tunes,
See I collect antiques from my old mother's trunk,
It embodies all her youth and truth.

I collect antiques from my grandmother's old family album,
Her favourite cup and saucer attached to my throat –
I still taste her essence every time I swallow my pride.
I remember a woven mat she created as precision of
her wrinkles toned us to sleep from her beautiful lullaby songs.
See I collect antiques from my grandmother's sewing machine.
Every prick of a needle stitched us to life every time poverty wounded us.
She knew hunger pangs from our eyes even if our innocent giggles marveled
her to perfection.

Her earrings pendant; filled with rainbow of charms as pearls and rubies –
Her favourite stone tanzanite; she would match it with silver linings of
clouds. Her dancing stance fused with algorithms of tortoise
she moves with a steady pace of the Kamikaze current.

Every morning her smile comes with nothing but truth as it lies in her face
Like morning dew, I collect antiques from my grandmother's mirror,

Her powder coded smile never fade as writings behind reflection still resonates in us every time we in search of ourselves.
Manifestation equivalent of heaven, she smiled even when
her breath was smiling at Pearly gates.

I still collect antiques so my grandmother's light can keep me in.

Tshediso Seroki

Antique: a collectable item with value because of its age; **boulders**: stones; **algorithms**: inventions; **Kamikaze:** self-destructing

TO PAMELA

Come to me but only with a smitten heart,
And I shall open mine before you depart;
Or say the magic words but within a prose
And say something about the scent of the rose.
The love that from your heart still grows
Must not die as the envious wind blows;
But if there's anything I'd ask you to do,
I would never ask you to be untrue.
I blow you late a goodnight kiss,
To show how much love in me there is;
But guilty of love and anger, your soul draws back –
Whether too little or too much, my love shan't slack.
My soul tells the heart, the heart tells the mind
That love is so cute but love is so blind;
Anarchy of thoughts, love and pride, all bemused –
There's no love as proper as mine to remain abused.
But be kind, I would never dare distraught thee
As I hope that you'll soon and forever be with me;
Be just and bid me welcome into your life –
And hand me joy by accepting to be my wife.
No feeling of love from me to you shall withered be;
Say not that I said it not without courtesy or glee,
Because ever since I told you that I love you, and swore,
You've scourged me more than you've ever done before.

Choene Semenya

Anarchy: chaos; **bemused**: confused, **distraught**: hurt, make sad, upset;
scourged: punished; **envious**: jealous; **slack**: feeble, weakens; **shan't**: shall not

ABOVE ODDS

I want to touch your soul to soul
but our skin tones keep colliding against each other like destructive race,
restricted by religion we ended up strangers.
You pulled west while looking for my strings attached to the east
Where I learnt art of my kind.

Your family reciting Christian hymns,
Mine burning Incense and calling ancestral names.
We follow the path of family ways, while our faces look down hoping to
find each other in our empty prayers.
We ate each other's hearts to keep each other against Odds.

Tshediso Seroki

LOVE, BE MY FRIEND!

O dear love, be my friend, even with thine name tarnished –
Being called conniving and deluding, for I know thou art not;
And all those whom of thou contented art, like I, forget not,
Abhor not, true love I address you, yet many sayst thou hast vanished.
From heart how I plead, that but with thee mayst I celebrate,
Friendship and amity of extraordinary pleasance and delight,
Much pleasance – sweet love of life, be never out of my sight;
This is my dearest plea, because I know thou art obedient to fate.
Thou art noble from noble wealth – I know thou art not perished,
Thou art not dreadful, thou art not despicable – O, bless me along;
And dost thou not beset me for I have never done thou wrong.
Love, I love you! from childhood I learnt thou art what I cherished;
Declare me blessed with fortune that even desolation cannot destroy
And whilst thou dost, forget not but to plethora me with incessant joy.

Choene Semenya

Conniving and deluding: manipulative and deceiving; **abhor**: hate,
loathe; **amity**: peace, harmony; **pleasance**: pleasure; **despicable**: evil;
beset: torture, punish; **desolation**: despair; **plethora**: surfeit, offer in
extreme excess; **incessant**: continuous

DARKNESS IS ETERNAL

Universes reside where darkness stays forever.
It is said Darkness birth light
Yet many contradictions keep painting darkness evil.

Darkness is the soundproof of light
Where body scales shift their purpose delight,
No patience keeps it's steadiness than darkness.
Every molecule in the body gets life out of Darkness,
It is said the human body is equivalent manifestation
of galaxies and constellations.

We give light credit and dishonour the light,
broken pens and pencils shape the edges for the next Fight.
Silence resides in darkness,
Anger plays hide and seek in Light.
History keeps moving and times are changing yet
Darkness hides life from enlightened ones,
For they don't honour life they take with their guns.

Rest in Peace when darkness leaves light in Pieces –
Coffins for bodies in search for life,
curtain of life wrapped in darkness where shapes of stars reside.
We don't see with our eyes when the seeing is colour blind.
Remove blind folders for your room is dark and faith is light;
Travel your path by faith and not by sight.

Our suitcases full of sunshine and light of the cosmos
we are in pursuit of light we forget from within.
From our fears of darkness we dig out dead bodies of our past
and create Frankensteins to our possible dreams.

We honour the light to scare away our fears,
yet darkness knows our tears.
When existence was naked, darkness was in existence.
Darkness our origins, where all light begins.

Honour your darkness; understand your light,
Your fear for darkness move you away from you.
Drapes around your lips ascend to the deep of darkness when
The gates of your mouth opens
To speak down to darkness.

See. Storms come and go.

Natural disasters come and live their mark into the ruins.
Yet Darkness knows to give hope when it regurgitates stars
back into the sky. Look at the night with a smile
And honour the darkness.

Tshediso Seroki

I DREAMT IT ALL

I know that I shall meet a pretty someone
Somewhere in the shops across the mall;
Those that I date now I do not love at all,
The lips that I kiss now I do it all for fun;
My life is driven by dreams and fate,
My love life is without honesty or sate,
But no part of you could understand me well
Or know what I feel or know where I dwell.
Nor guilt, nor situation oblige me to lie,
Nor predicaments, bade me to sigh,
A lonesome soul bereft of delight –
I, who sleeps alone, by the night;
I dreamt it all: the lady, the date, and the day,
The months to come will demise my solitude away
Because all that I dreamt is all that I ever sought,
There shall be no more stress to feed my thought.

Choene Semenya

Sate: satisfaction; **oblige**: cause; **predicaments**: troubles, difficulties; **bereft of delight**: that lacks joy or gladness; **solitude**: loneliness

LET'S MAKE LOVE

Pick a Crayon, Let Me pick Mine.

Let me draw how our foreplay is going to be like,
There will be lights on the floor as candles to lead our steps as
We will learn to find each other in the darkest hour.
I will come close to you as your voice will be
The flame that attracts me like a moth –
No! Wait! Let me erase the first part.
There will be no music on the background but
only melodies of our heartbeats.

My Left hand closer to your chest!

Let me unzip my fears.
My lips tremble as I want to collect life from your kiss.
Wait! That's not right; your red dress will suite the mood.
The staccato in the air creates keys as if your demon is calling mine.
Your perfume pulled me out of my span to spin around this
Thought of us to and fro.
I lost my sense in search of your flow.
Kiss on the neck to find where voices you speak reside,
My palms holding your body like celo, with heavenly strings;
To remind me that you are the reason for my living dreams.
WET palms breaking sweat, pores gasp for air, Pause!

Let's Start Again!

This time I will start on your left ear to summon these whispers
To move colony of ants on your spine, divine movement as body speaks
tantra.
Skin covered in glitter as body chemistry precipitates the mood,
Wait, let me close my eyes and imagine what it's like
To draw with melting crayon on hot paper; this is no foreplay –
Let's play for the senses to twist tornados within
Clustered chests as we breath as one.

Look what this crayon has done – it drew reality from thin air,
for I saw rivers flowing like your natural hair.
I was once broken stuff my cracks with pieces of your smile,
Listen to my deep and discover river Nile.
Paint me colour of life and let me live beneath your skin.

Tshediso Seroki

THE RELINQUISHER'S MONOLOGUE

To relinquish or not to relinquish, that is the question;
whether 'tis nobler in the mind to suffer
An everlasting emotional torture of pretentious infatuations,
Or just to let it all go
And by opposing, shatter them. To withstand, to relax;
Nay more; and by not relaxing, I mean feeling belittled
Losing my integrity when she eternally rejects me.
Losing my voice when she dares not to listen;
My breath wasted at an ignorant person:
To be with her; 'tis a dream I wish to fulfill: to withstand, to relax;
To accomplish: perchance to win her over; ay, there's the ring.
And to that desperately needed break there comes time to meditate;
She must give in: there stands my reward
That makes the loss of my integrity worthwhile.

Choene Semenya

Infatuations: feelings of intense passion for someone, especially for a short time; **belittled** made to feel small; **meditate**: think

YOUR BEATIFIC SMILE

It's your beatific smile
That makes me weep
it's a flicker of trust in your eye
Another feeling in your heart
it's an unsullied love conquering the air

But chiefly
it's your beatific smile in your smiling
that makes me weep.

Choene Semenya

Unsullied: pure; not spoiled; **conquering**: overcoming

STORY UNTOLD

In stories of my distant relatives,
A young girl's innocence ripped in the presence of her parents,
Her thighs like calvary she bleeds.

Now she moved to the city to make ends meet,
Her body now is like a hospital, between her thighs lies a mortuary,
Men go in there to die.
She smiles – death has many names.
She is now a young woman learning the only education given by rebel
Captains as her village caught fire.
She still burns.
'Tis not how she envisioned her story would turn,
She then hides in her skin for as long as she can.

Tshediso Seroki

THE THRENODY OF A BEREFT FRIEND

Here cries a young woman who recently lost her friend;
She was angry with her friend – she scolded her rage, her rage did end.
A voice from the dead spat: "Friend! I know what I did was a great mess;
Profuse apologies –and to be honest, I wouldn't ask for your pardon unless
I was at peace. Where I are it is evermore burning and there's no getting old;
Yet there's only a way in and no way out – no food, no water, nor feeling bold.
Apart from that though, I know that my death had put you through a lot of pain,
But there's definitely no need to cry; I won't return, for there's no dying again.
Now listen: 'til the sun sheds its tears, just keep on singing our favourite song;
And at any rate, the lamentation shan't recur; yet the song will keep you strong."

Choene Semenya

Scolded: reprimanded, rebuked; **lamentation**: an expression of great sadness and disappointment

BLACK MEN ENDANGERED SPECIES!

And their stories start with death, from Sharpeville to Marikina massacre –
Story starts with *They started a fight* out of panic white men shot black men
dead. Fees must fall, tear gas pushing propaganda
When fathers holding guns shoot their daughters and Sons.

My black fathers have been filling up Shebeens and liquor stores,
When shacks catch fire as argument breaks through thin iron sheets,
Black labels RIVERS to cross over sober habits.
An acquaintance forgotten by time,
remembered himself only at a sip of vodka.

Rhinos have campaigns,
My black fathers become pains as they hurt every
Syllable left of their Ego.
Black men's story always begins with death.

Heroes don't die natural death, they either see police vans,
Or farmhouses where their skeletons are food for soil.
My black men are stolen from their rituals and customs
To be stuffed with bullshit like Rug dolls.

Prison walls painted with painted memory of fallen angels,
Death sentence has never missed a black man.
When hospital beds are full its black men with lungs
Decomposed from sniffing asbestos in the mines but
Who cares, as long as its black man nothing is wrong.
It's business as usual nothing personal.

Black men are endangered species man –
and there are no heroes,
Mothers blaming them,
sons disrespecting them,
and daughters disowning them,

My Fathers are endangered species man.
Not Even tuxedos can suit their wounded egos,
Not even briefcases can mind their businesses.
Shackles are in many forms, and weird norms.
Black men have been dying, and many we bury every weekend
when tents tend to the wounded –

We Bleed.
We bury our own six feet debt in,
Credit cards exhausted we die many deaths
Before exiting skeletal prisons.
See my kind is in danger.
Broken sons can't hold where fathers held for
They don't know Them.
Remember no man lives to die,
Yet black men have known death like graveyards.
Black men don't cry no more they act their Pain.

Tshediso Seroki

Propaganda: Information to mislead

TO SILENT ONES

Tales are for heroes to be remembered,
lips like a machete cutting words to silent tones.
Crimes of injustice prevailing when the righteous lock themselves
behind high walls of their guilt;
Silence of the good is the same as atrocities of the wicked.

Tshediso Seroki

Atrocities: Cruelness, offensiveness

TO CARON

You, the love of my life, beauty is precisely what you define –
You are the rose of the valleys that possesses a scent so divine;
And your eyes so tender, far more like the moon glistering bright,
So is your love unto me, not half so comparable at day or at night.
Your lips, O my sweet, as the stars across the clouds, beautiful
Than the lips of those whose hobbies are to tell lies so awful –
And your smile is kind, as though all joys were vested in you;
And your touch is benign, when I lie in your arms fearing dew.
And your voice is liquid, could hardly breathe when I hear you sing,
And your tangy kiss, and O, the velvet of your skin! What a gentle thing! –
Like the softest sand of the deepest sea, it stimulates shipment of sentiments;
With a plethora of love, and dignity I must say 'My poem, –this is how it ends!'
But beshrew me, I never wish to lo and behold my soul dissever from that of yours,
And awake at midnight, and say: 'The love is over and gone, or perhaps even worse!'

Choene Semenya

Dissever: separate, be apart; **benign**: harmless, safe

TO MY SONS

I have been a boy until your arrival –
Time has been freezing moments for me to start teaching;

I stand before you as naked as truth
Lessons of fatherhood are learned
But being a good father is earned.

I may speak from a tongue full of dust,
When you of age I will teach you about trust.
Never raise your hand to your beloved
Just as I have never raised mine to your mother.
You will grow to see flaws but love each other.

Learn to speak from a clear mind
For anger is blinder –
Master the art of forgiving,
And give your life pure meaning.
Love without expectations,
Learn to be happy with lamentations.

Where wrong, apologise with meaning
For there will be days for kneeling.
Prayer is the remedy for unseen wars
Rejoice in life at hand than past scars.

Live,
be playful find love,
make mistakes and learn from them;
Most of all when you love,
Love without regret or as though you have never been hurt.
Treat everyone with respect no matter young or old –

Find your firmament and learn to be bold.
Keep these lessons for I never knew how to Father,
I'm learning to shape you.

From
Your Father.

Tshediso Seroki

ABOUT MY EX-GIRLFRIEND

O this lady, I once thought I was so over her –
But whenever I see her pass,
I sigh with the swinging grass;
Believe you me I tremble, as if kissing her.

And when I see her hugging with another guy,
I get jealous, and she'd only smile and look away;
Her smile is still charming me I must say –
I guess there's still chemistry 'tween she and I.

Even though, I doubt she feels the same.
And trust me when I say, I learnt a lot from our jilt;
I learnt never to decide by virtue of anger or guilt –
Or tell my girlfriend I'm tired of love's war-game.

Even when I am dolorous and in despair,
Or I feel deprived of the love I know I deserve –
Just in case, I always keep some love out for reserve;
Dare not break her heart and go seek love elsewhere.

Like I did to this prepossessing lady over here;
Who was always soft when she talked,
And very much classy when she walked,
Though her body is slim and her accent so sheer.

All that I did was because I couldn't compete
With all the cute guys out there;
For I know life and love ain't fair –
Chiefly for okes who wear not fancy label at their feet.

A lot has happened, but I erred to reckon I'd stopped loving her ever;
And I know she too thinks she loves me no more,
But she is still in love with me as I am with her, I know –
For we make an integral part of each other, altho' now she's with Denver.

And whenever I bump into her and she looks at me,
Somehow I feel as if I'm dreaming –
That I would hear her screaming:
'Ross, O Ross come to me –please come back to me.'

I think of her almost every morning when I wake up –
I remember how I used to wipe her tears when she cried;
And how badly I used to feel whenever she noticed I lied –
And nightly ere I sleep, always I wish not to think of her at sunup.

Yet I think all is in the past, it matters not now –
I will write her a love poem with humorous stanzas,
And invite her out to lovers' extravaganzas;
And offer her all the love and happiness I can bestow.

And then I will ask for forgiveness and for peace,
I will do whatever it takes even if it means calling myself a schmuck,
I will request fate to fate me success and bring me luck –
I believe we're a match made in heaven and we can make a new lease.

Well the truth is foolproof and humble: I miss her just a lot;
And even after the pain I've occasioned her I say, still –
I dote upon her and that's the way I always shall feel,
In spite of this bewilderment that goes against my thought.

Choene Semenya

Jilt: ending or termination of a romantic relationship; **dolorous**: expressing sadness; **deprived**: denied of something; **prepossessing**: attractive; **erred**: made a mistake; **integral**: essential, important; **bestow**: give; **schmuck**: a person who is stupid, idiot

JAKE

He wanted to find his way between cracks as he sniffed white lines,
pop of a vein next to a junky urge.
Skin picking itches, he scratches so hard,
Perhaps he needs another sniff of unholy dust,
Perhaps he wants to peel off his sins,
For he can't breathe away his edges of addiction.
His nose wants more, his skin itches some more.
He fights his demons in rehab centers day in, day out.
Every day to him starts with a greeting:
'Hi my Name is Jake.'

Tshediso Seroki

THE STREET KID'S LAMENT

The end of me: To sleep, a way to unimaginable bad dreams;
And never to wake up to earthly life that's what it means.
And to miss the quietude nature of cold nights,
Away from the glimmer and sight of the street lights.
To putrefy slowly and smell malodorous yet
With people being so quick to forget –
A litany of flies buzzing all over me,
Ensuring that I do not demise peacefully...
And no one comes to check on my lifeless corpse in the sun,
For they have deserted me long before I was even one.
Just like when I rose every dawn from card boxes alone in the morning mist,
Thinking what I would do for the day and everything would be on the list.
Begging, marauding, puffing glue, but bathing was never part of them;
Or preparing for school. And I would seek grub, for hunger would then be firm.
But now finally the vultures are coming to get me off the hook –
They'll lacerate me the way I used to read about them in the book.
Leastways I am not gonna be perished or parched or ailing or famished again.
But I'll probably be free of life of servitude in spite of exhaustion and pain –
High above to the kingdom of Heaven I am going without lament but dirt;
And with dark Sicilian secrets hidden in the pocket of my old spent shirt.
I'll not make funny sounds when hunting for a better place to hide.
Nobody must hear me, the dead young man with a hurt pride –
O poor little me, piteous, simple-hearted and too young to be old,
The sun will not help me find a place where my life will unfold.

Choene Semenya

Putrefy: decay; **malodorous:** smelling terrible; **demise:** die; **marauding:** going round in places in search for things to steal and people to attack; **lacerate:** cut skin or flesh severely; **servitude:** slavery; **Sicilian:** frightening; **unfold:** continue

LOVE LIKE THIS

Emotions for Trampolines,
Hearts for Jumping Castles,
Flexible walls, when diaphragm plays catch with missing air;
When beats await another smash against decaying ribs.
Wait, an inhalation lungs black out to confuse demons within . . .
See, love has never sounded like a poltergeist moving things,
From palpitations to butterflies in the stomach;
Something sinister about falling for space where meaning
Of events is out of focus.

Names things to change spirit of things,
Faces keep changing phases like rubric cube.
See, make up can't hide facade for good.
Tongue curling away words needed,
Lips sealed for something blissful,
Silence is golden I know now.
If you want to know just ask me how?

Tshediso Seroki

Poltergeist:(German for "noisy ghost") is a type of ghost or other supernatural entity which is responsible for physical disturbances, such as loud noises and objects being moved or destroyed

GOODNIGHT

Goodnight to the love of my life,
Goodnight to my haven of solace.
Caron, oh thou –my prospective wife,
I know that sleep can be such a beautiful place.

The moon shines on the side of your bed,
And in your joyous sleep sense the dream;
By now the darkness is dead
And your name I wish I could scream.

The day was long, the day was cold;
Full of empty cries, full of fancy lies –
You've been young, but now you are old
To bear the lie that so your joy denies.

The night to you can only be fair,
And oh, sweet, here's goodnight;
All that your tormented soul can repair,
Do you feel this, – this delight?

This delight that so heals the mind,
Warm, candid and kind and plain;
This breeze that sweeps the past behind,
And myself wishing to kiss your lips again?

I wish the stars could bring you peace;
I wish you luck to keep you strong,
That all banes against you may cease
And a sweet love encoded in a song.

My voice is hoarse but still I'll sing
And my first line would go like:
'To me baby, you are just everything. . .'
Dear, I know you already miss my bike.

But I'll miss you deeply through the night,
And remember how I mended your heart,
      And long shall wait I, the lonely knight –
Whose phrases to your ears are always pure art.

      The sky is rich with a constellation of stars;
Though the night can never be so bright –
      Even if we adjoin the stars with the lights of cars,
O Sweetie, I just wanted to bid you Goodnight.

Choene Semenya

BROKEN CUPS

Wars framed within our state of minds,
Battle drums tamed where tears reside,
Houses losing heads, family trees heading to poverty streams.
HIV/AIDS on the other hand shattering dreams,
Schools are more redundant than shebeen tables –
Turns to turn around, what we know to what we don't;
Drinking sorrows on squashed throats never ease
the pain of unemployment.

Upon broken cups heroes wear medals of honour
When they descend to six feet to compose songs in their names.
Trophies are tombstones and epiphanies;
When mothers are widows and children keep
searching for their fathers return
through broken windows...

Broken cups are mended by sands of time falling
on yawning wounds.

Tshediso Seroki

Epiphanies: Revelations

CONFESSION OF THE MANIAC

I get this recurring feeling that I'll die soon;
And my death will be beyond the smile of the moon.
For in the discreet of nightfall I'd always be out to kill;
Boasting my hefty bloodlust for killing was my greatest thrill.
If I could I would, but return to life all the souls I'd slain;
Or request for amnesty in return for death without pain.
Across the mind I could recollect victims in sorrowful joy;
But I didn't give a toss – I was seventeen, I was still a boy.
Rags and riches I faded away, but then beauteous ones managed to flee;
Though life was a pleasance yet not everything was as I wished it could be.
Already my unspeakable intentions were fairly known to the night;
For plenitude days at dusk, I'd always do evil that set my heart alight.
Many I menaced and scared, and guilt haunt me will forever,
And there shall be blood stained on my hands forever and ever.

Choene Semenya

Slayer: killer; **maniac**: madman, a person who behaves in an extremely dangerous, wild and stupid way; **beyond the smile of the moon**: of extreme barbarity, very cruel; **hefty**: plenty, big; **slain**: killed; **rags and riches**: poor and rich people; **pleasance**: an old English word for pleasure; **plenitude**: plenty, abundant; **menaced**: threatened, **amnesty**: forgiveness

LETTER TO THE HOLY BIBLE

Thou shalt not kill:
Mass graves to bury the truth who made the Law?
Slaves to obey their masters,
such words for the holy book that promotes injustice;
Black book blacker pages whiter who teaches
salvation when bones of my forefathers keep
turning on their shadow closets.

In the beginning God said let's create man in our image,
Why Jesus now white,
Or is it shift of control on my lineage?
Curse of Cain or the sin of the fallen caused
God to flood the earth he created?

Sodom and Gomorrah burnt to ashes as Genesis of genetics
Was Adam and Eve;
Not Adam and Steve the forbidden fruit still stuck on Adams throat.
Thou shalt not covert, convert them to Christians
if they don't believe impale them on a stake
and leave them hanging.

Lynching necks to snap the reason out of their body experience,
love yourself as you love thy neighbour,
yet we build high walls to secure the properties and
never to feed the starving neighbour.
Lot's wife turned into an ornament of salt,

Wounds on my forefathers' graves stuffed with
all bitter lies to wrap our ways to extinction.

Explain this: ask and you shall be given,
whips and shackles to take the land and replaced with man-made laws.
Egypt to tell a tale of Moses beyond The Red Sea,
Wait, Jesus a born of virgin such miracle when the reason
beyond biology and science cannot prove this fiction,
History of Horus is mummified in
The tombs of Khemet who is lying?

Tale says Jesus turned water to wine,
He walked on water then the merchant ship came
to steal village warriors out Africa.
Create wine to seek why serpent slithered in the grapevines of Eden,
Even Eve couldn't keep her thighs closed
For defilement gets your body lose its sense.
Oh well, Manna from heaven sounds like charity case
to get our thoughts misplaced.
Wait; let's talk of ten plaques . . .

Starting with the last plaque,
Can God administer death when he created Man in His Image?
I guess angel of death was Michael the dumb angel,
how do you kill innocent kids to prove a point?
Now that explains why it is said kids will be punished
for the atrocities of parents.
Poor us children of lost scrolls,
heirs and prodigal sons to shackled fathers.

I hope this letter reaches the Vatican on time,
So that the pope releases shackles off my people.
'If following the footfalls of my forefather is
Foolish, then that I rather be.'

Tshediso Seroki

Mummified: preserved

SUNRISE AND SUNSET

The dawn broke, and the sun rose,
And the birds sang of dew,
And dew disappeared in the sun.

The grass halted drooping,
As the weight of dew died away,
And the sun kept on shining.

At eventide, when sun set
And the birds roosted,
And the dew fell again:

The grass continued to slouch,
As the weight of dew ravished again,
And consummation came –
the vanity of nightfall.

Choene Semenya

Halted: stopped; **droop**: bend or hang down limply; **roosted**: rested, slept;
ravished: overwhelmed, overpowered; **vanity**: pride of yourself

BULLET SHELLS

Memories falling like broken chandeliers,
History written from falling tears,
Bodies missing, found with bullet holes stuck in the skulls.
Dead men can't speak for their course of course,
because nothing dead can speak life.

Grounds in Marikina holds tales of dead men
waging war for minimum wage,
These bullet shells stuffed with heavy burdens of
families who lost their bread winners;
Abundance redundant to ornaments of misery,
when streets are loaded with shells waiting to crack.

Suicide on the rise,
Cops crashing course causing cacophony cease at the end of smoking gun.
These guns are loaded with pain, shells shaping scars leaving
Wills empty with beneficiaries.
See, shells keep cracking brilliantly like
Glass hearts smashed against the wall.

Hitmen dressed in broken armour,
morning brings saddest hour.
Orphans often lose kisses and hugs,
gangsters grooming gang full of slugs.
These shells are shape shifter; at times
They are white powder waiting for nostrils to sniff the
Path of fallen heroes on heroine.

History on repeat
death on our feet,
Lungs dark in smoke of fallen shells;
We struggle to breath fresh air as shells still stuck in our inhalations.

At 21gunshot salute, we bury soldiers whose songs
keep landing on deaf ears.
Aluta Continúa!!

Tshediso Seroki

Cacophony: uncontrollable noise; **Aluta Continúa**: Spanish word
meaning Struggle continues

ADRIANA JONES

Whenever Adriana Jones went down the mall,
We fellas on the streets lasciviously ogled at her:
She was a lady in and beyond and about all,
Calm, adroit and her breed was fairly rare.

She was different from all of us, with a sophisticated pride
That came from deep her wealthy life; and the blazers
She wore were couture. She was voluptuous from side
To side: and she had all the money to spend on extravaganzas.

And she was always sensationally attired,
And she was always kind when she spoke;
And her lips looked too smooth to be real, desired
By every man of family and every young bloke.

And she was ravishing —yup, most ravishing than a queen —
And majestically studied at a fancy finishing school:
In all, we people thought that she was a lady to preen
To make us wish we were also that beautiful and that cool.

Hence on we wished, and awaited her nuptial day;
For she was aesthetic —a perfect exhibition of God's art.
And so Adriana Jones, one impeccable Valentine's Day,
Went home and pierced the blade of a knife through her heart.

Choene Semenya

Lasciviously ogled: lustfully looked; **adroit**: delicate; **breed**: type, kind;
sophisticated: proudly knowledgeable about things that we thought were
socially important; **couture**: of expensive design; **ravishing**: extremely
beautiful; **preen**: admire, love looking at; **nuptial**: wedding; **impeccable**:
perfect

CAN WE TAKE IT BACK?

Maybe I ran out of patience before learning texture of your smile,
Man carries to much pride under his skin,
You are the only beauty my eyes has ever seen.

It's been few weeks now since I mark your silence.
Your unsaid words still mark how you moved my center
as movement of earthquakes.

Can we take it back?

Maybe my ego weighed my emotions for a broken man,
I hope to move closer to your silence,
and listen to your heart beats I know
it may be late for letters and flatters.

Can we take it back?

To holding hands and singing along
Karaoke nights.
I miss your singing along,
Your voice coded in angels tone.

Can we take it back?

Many a time I spoke of world beneath worlds,
you took mine wrapped in your with celestial
skins refining texture of happiness.

Can we take it back?

To ideas of life
Beyond these coffins for bodies.

Tshediso Seroki

Karaoke: interactive

DEAR GRANNY

Dear granny, we shall always remember you each day;
You've fostered us, and so much of you each can say –
If but life was a crystal, we'd seen through it this dreadful fate,
And learnt to espouse the plight in advance that you are late.
You were weary of ailments and lethargies that had you slain,
But from a dream how we wish we would awake to see you again,
And jest with you and laugh with you and rejoice with laughter –
As you narrate to us the family history of the early 60s before and after.
Oh, Gogo, our beloved –How much in God we pray and quest
That your disembodied soul be saved only with the celestial best;
Treasured shall your absence from this barbaric life in eternity be –
And honour shall at your interment prevail as we lament thee.
As withered from this planet your life becomes, we accept now that it ends,
And all we hope for as your bereft, is that you betimes make new friends.

Choene Semenya

Fostered: nurtured; **espouse**: accept, agree to live with something; **ailments and lethargies**: illness and body weaknesses; **disembodied**: separated from the body; **celestial**: heavenly; **barbaric**: cruel, **interment**: funeral, burial; **bereft**: mourning, grieving; **betimes**: quickly

THINGS I WANT TO FORGET (PART1)

Nights take longer than normal
as traces gets lost within infinite spaces,
The fortune was read in stars and misinterpreted on
My heavens – My skull became the archives for dark magic.

As night falls in rivers flow follows my footsteps,
I took a leap of faith outta my skeletal prison to discover my freedom.
These poems are mundane to a celestial being,
I kept echoes for as long as I can remember.
These skeletons in my closet have voices,
the deeper the night the harder the whispers.

My schizophrenic flashbacks keep pulling me back,
to my frame where scars and wounds grow like lilies and dandelions –
I replaced my iris for clocks everytime I blink no second passes by my eye;
I can see vividly now that the beast got tamed by broken roars,
cords from my voice suspended my silence like chandeliers,
I replaced my skin for paper sheets for every time I scratch
I Scribe.

These poems are tattoos from within,
I know every time I break my heart it grows back as a poem.
Relationships are boats I timeously wreck them for a reason I don't know,
At night I astroproject to seek my soul.
Maybe God is showing me a world beyond these
Wrecks I'm constantly trying to fix.

Perhaps this poem is
My silent matra maneuvering,
This is a Poem not about Me.

Tshediso Seroki

Astroproject: travel a soul, spirit or any part of the mind to a location other than physical location or to imagine such a travel; **schizophrenic**: relating mental instability

THINGS I WANT TO FORGET (PART2)

I want to forget about race and racism.
I want to forget about boundaries and barriers.
I want to forget about hosts and carriers.

I want to forget about broken hearts,
angry lovers,
and rebellious children;
Broken homes,
dying off-springs,
I want to forget about many things that are unforgettable.

How do I forget when media keeps reminding me
of my place in this world?
When poverty strikes, it is families who live from scraps.
I want to forget about how much men are broken
but societal norms keep building walls to keep us(Men)
out of our misguided children.

Time heals scars yet mine only pack dust when
my flaws are perpetual to my ageing number.
I want to forget about how we became villains –
our children have estranged us,
Lineage of broken generation.

I JUST want to FORGET.

Tshediso Seroki

MOURN ME NOT

Mourn me not when I am dead,
Gone to a place remote from this land;
When thou canst no more say:
'I love thee in just this way;'
Nor tell me jokes, nor kiss my hand.
Reminisce of me nevermore when in bed,

Just know that I & life were never friends;
Recall that life was just my living —that's all.
So, the moon shone and declared my passing;
My body lifeless, for the moon saw me grassing
My days with prayer, but that was just a holy call
And no one should weep when my life ends.

Like the period of autumn in every leasing year,
Bid me farewell when transitory be my lifespan, and —
Dost thou not mourn me, dost thou not mock me
Nor sing praises for me like a silent sea;
If such there be hope that I've not gone to a foreign land
When my blest soul enters the Pearly Gates, beware,

I shall sleep not mournful but better in my grave!
Knowing that my family and friends osculate me goodbye,
That with songs sincere they've only compared me with me,
That they rejoice with me as I travel to paradise, and be
Glad that Heaven will revive and revitalize me, so that I
As I die be the best that I could ever be with Heaven my cave.

Choene Semenya

Remote: far; **reminisce**: recollect, think about happy times of the past;
grassing: betraying; **transitory**: short-lived; **the Pearly Gates**: the gates
of Heaven; **my cave**: my house

IN BLANKET OF DEATH WE LIVE

Garment giving cosmos it's beauty,
reality walks a mile for stars to shoot to the ground.
ZODIAC signs life to constellations,
a day of reckoning comes before
Life springs out of frozen further.

No one bothers to ask the whereabouts of Supernovae,
but many wish upon stars B for luck.
Beginners beg upon candles for prayers
yet no one ask the flame where it's burnt,
Of course no one cares on ash that burnt for
Misconstrued elders' stories.

A push to break bones and tear a muscle,
birth places are always bloody to mark where infants wrestled with death;
See, they come as spirits clenching fists.
A connection on umbilical cord suspends life into the air.
Stars are chandeliers blue of skies
Roof that house firmament of the deep.

He ripped off innocence out of his ageing skin;
Gueno broke all the laws of life to forge death in his flesh –
For birth to make sense death must not be in past tense.
Bodies pilling dust of the graves, six feet live eternal names.
Bore–agains keep dying an empty death in search for grace in God,
the irony is denial of self – now that's odd.

Hand of God not too short to save you,
yet hands of time folds memories to galvanise molecules
of self to move closer to life;
Eyes for paper sheets, visions of blind man writes monologues
To temple housing scars.

See, death is not a death sentence but abandoned dreams
That keep playing hide and seek at sleeping giants.

Tshediso Seroki

ZODIAC: an area of the sky centered upon the ecliptic, the apparent
path of the Sun across the celestial sphere over the course of the year;
misconstrued: misinterpreted; **galvanise**: stimulate

SONNET TO HIJACKERS

You've frigging blundered and shot dead my loving wife;
You could've just taken her vehicle and spared her life.
O but you cold-hearted hijackers just tell me why –
Just tell me why you slain her while you still live on by;
How the heck do you live with yourselves? How do you?
When you think of the pain I must be going through;
The least I have of her now is the memories we made awhile
But you have taken away my everyday hope (her morning smile) –
And there's still a lot about her you took I cannot define
Like the fact that she and I were an inextricable intertwine;
At least that's what I thought, until you came into the picture,
And took one of us and disrupted our auspicious future.
Beshrew me, for life in hell is where you belong, behind bars,
Where you can hardly feel the sun and can barely see the stars.

Choene Semenya

Inextricable intertwine: inseparable bond; **auspicious**: promising;
beshrew me: dammit

EDUCATION WE KNOW

We have been taught to die,
As long as your color black, die –
In screams of dead heroes our lives
Mean nothing as long as we die.

Education is the key to lock away black outside
To experience the bitter truth of democracy.
The darker the berry the sweeter the juice a myth,
Remains of black lives still stuck in our memories
like teargas on decaying lungs.

We have been taught to about guns
and disappearing good sons.
We have buried heroes beneath the dust of our gravel roads.
Promising stars shine for time being and die amidst lost talent
and lack of Education how to save.
We want to save money than our innate talents,
To invest in fragments of foreign imposters not our
Blossoming Dreams.

We have been taught to call ourselves less human and self-hate –
See, the black lives are under siege.
We have been given terms like black on black crime is on the rise,
Forgetting whose ideas instilled hate on black society.
We have been sent to school to become statistics generated by Education,
We are still taught of hard work when corrupt officials and politicians
Get richer while graduates remain unemployed.
Who is fooling who?

We have been taught to call each other names.
I know deep down that short skirt you are looking and
Seeking a goddess misinterpreted, hiding away your skin
under make up doesn't give you the path to self;
The anger, the fear and bitterness,
We are products of second hand freedom.

We were taught to kill our own,
To gain trust of those who intend our submission.
We are still taught about Kingdom of God
When earth is not a place to seek salvation.

No!
These teachings have labelled leaders of our liberation villains.

Tshediso Seroki

FORESTS BECOME DESERTS

Forests become deserts
at winter, after less rains,
smeared with dry aridness,
the shriveled tare faint with hunger...

Deep, deep, deep
is the midwinter's howling winds above them!

Oh, why are they not
as once we believed they were,

Withered flowers,
their au naturel hue disappeared in the sun?

Choene Semenya

Aridness: dryness; **au naturel hue**: natural colour

WHERE ARE YOU NOW?

Do you remember where you lost your map leading back to self?
In pursuit of acceptance and sense of belonging you lost God
and found wilderness behind fake smiles and facade.

Have you done to someone what you want them to do unto to you?
In mist of hate love comes to be true,
No matter what you have been through.
Dismember their compass; put your spiritual radar
if you are in search of what can be.

In the mist of broken hearts,
failing bodies don't collapse to hate,
Yes, many a time we get angry and with our
Tongues we do more harm than Good.

Where are you now?

Have you found yourself on bended knees?
Our mothers live there;
Their faces know only tears when they say grace for our names.
Our fathers have been breaking down since dawn of mankind,
we have known only our fathers love on our mother's bruised faces.

Where are you now?

Have you broken down walls around your heart?
For someone is willing to love and cherish you.
Let go of your burden, it's too much to carry like
hunchback with deformed spines.
Behold what your chest is made out of;
Skeletons have been doing sex change.
Many Adams are reborn as Adelaides, victims of unheard screams.
No! We can't keep holding on what used to be our pain –
Discarded all your spades for many graves we have dug for each other.

Wear lenses for telescopes and see people for who they really are,
not their circumstances.
Privileges have no boundaries yet we forget
We are made in the image of God the eternal flame.

WE have been here before.

Tshediso Seroki

OLD MAN TROUBLED (SONNET)

The night breeze is thick and too cold,
It makes me feel so pale and so, so old.
The darkness is so pure and most deep,
And it gives me a reason not to sleep.
The conquered moon is plain without a sheath,
It makes me so scared I can hardly breathe.
The jaded stars are yet hanging limply and jocose,
And it gives me no hope but death so close.
Tall trees quiver like brooms sweeping the sky;
And it pains me so abysmal, but nay I shall not cry –
For now I'm so old and decrepit and close to die
I should sommer prepare myself to say goodbye,
To everyone that loved me throughout all my life
And ameliorated my solitude ever since I lost my wife.

Choene Semenya

Sheath: cover that fits closely for protection; **jaded**: tired, no longer wanting to continue doing something; **jocose**: humorous; **abysmal**: very deep; **nay**: no; **decrepit**: battered, weak

PUSH BACK

Life is a present full of many gifts;
Tears are frequencies from your pain when it hurts.
Your enemies plotted pain and downfall for you,
But in all this never hate yet always stay true.

Kindness is invincible, practice it.
You have opened doors of friendship to dine with broken friends –
Now look at knives at your back.
Walk away with silence and never look back.

Love is free, grudges are burdens.
Give love for no reason to receive it back,
Your chest has keys locking secrets of those you trust,
when you are between rock and hard surface no one aids fast.
Life is a class with continuous lessons.
You were hurt for all sinister reasons.

Steady your knees grounds have ears to listen no matter when your faith
lessens. Keep your head up, for sky is not the limit to look pass a facade,
Not every friend stays yet loyalty everywhere pays.

Tshediso Seroki

THRENODY FOR THE MARIKANA MINER'S WIFE

This poem is based on deaths of protestors of the Lonmin mine that transpired on 16 August 2012 in North West; platinum mine situated in Marikana, Rustenburg, South Africa. I wholeheartedly, with heartfelt condolences dedicate this poem to all families that lost their loved ones in that blood-spattered tragedy. I mourn with you their death. May their souls rest in peace!

They lived gaily together before the blood-curdling strike began.
He was her husband, the father of her kids – and a better man.
He was an operator at Lonmin mine and at home a breadwinner;
Notwithstanding he earned as little as though he was a mere cleaner.

He served among the discontented and bitter mob of Marikana mine;
To claim the wage he believed he deserved early in the sunrise shine –
Him and all those men there were fighting for what's morally theirs,
And not even a fraction of the salary earned by the local mayors.

He was a brave man – he merged the dolorous miners who pranced on their feet,
With fatal weapons in their dexterous hands as they marched on the sunny street.
Yet neglect struck them, by a guilt-ridden mine that overlooked its wrongs,
And so their protest unfolded, with sweat griming their faces whilst they sang their aching songs.

But that Thursday, Thursday what an ill-fated day with gobs of smoking gunfire;
Police scattered bullets where her husband made his stand; they executed her children's sire –
O Alas! And never did he return from a protest that turned into a perforce bloodbath,
After the fuming miners stirred a bedlam with judicious alibis that condoned their wrath.

But still, who was raring to listen? Who wished to be accounted responsible?
Who cared? When the world only saw a bunch of hooligans being
insensible –
Their economical issues unresolved, yet they were regarded a mass of
greed –
Poor mine workers labelled as unreasonable, and as unreasonable indeed.

Her husband was shot for God's sake; a good man who knew so well
the riches of this African land,
Exploited by a mine that made billions from his perpetual servitude
endured by the palms of his hand –
. . .and after the miners waited in vain for wage demands,
they eventuated a recalcitrant blood thirst fight;
The whole of the scene involved family men whose livid man-made
weapons were not willing to despair tearing their plight.

Oh yes, the police viciously fought back in case any question
is asked why these poor men died –
And her husband was amid those lifeless bodies lying on the gory
ground after the dust died away, because he too tried.
But oh regrettably –My mind wonders: WHO is gonna buy
his family every morning a bread,From today as future unfolds, now that
the police had shot a bullet through his head?

Choene Semenya

Discontented: unsatisfied, unhappy; **merged**: joined; **dexterous**: skillful;
aching: painful; **perforce**: unnecessary; **bedlam**: chaos; **judicious alibis**:
reasonable intentions, sensible reasons; **professed**: said; **industrious**:
hardworking; **perpetual servitude**: continuous slavery; **recalcitrant**:
uncontrollable; **livid**: very angry

LOVE LETTER FROM MARIKANA

Dear Mantwa

I have been in pursuit of things our dreams cannot complete,
I still keep our memories in a trunk you bought me on our first anniversary,
I still have your smiles to help me survive the cold winter nights,
I still remember our playful fights about Soweto derby.

How are our children?
I hope they are still learning *'Tsela ya sefapano'*.
Let them pray for me just as I'm praying for them every night.
How is our little daughter?
I can't wait to feel her tiny palms; harken to her innocent giggles.

I have been hearing talks from the shop stewards about salary increase;
I cannot wait for the talks to end – it's promising.
I can finally buy you a new washing machine.
Do you still watch the sunset on the hill when you have time?
If you don't, please do for, every sunset it's me
who goes underground like dying rays succumbing to nature.
I have learnt new dance moves, this time I will be the winner.

Your favorite song from Letta Mbulu's album gets me thinking:
'Not yet Uhuru' I think I understand now.
I eat every night.
There have been gun shots here and there is hope
they did not kill my friend Zama.
You know tribalism here in the belly of the beast.

How is our inquisitive neighbour, Dora?
I guess now she has found herself a man.
What happened to her previous drunkard of a taxi driver?
In fact, I don't think I wanna hear of it.

My love, I have been saving money for a holiday in Durban,
I can't wait for my feet to land on sands of the famous South Beach.

We will take many pictures, build many sand castles,
And dive into playful waves.
We will visit where fish and other season's creature reside.
They called that place aquarium,
I learnt the word in ABET English class.

My Queen, I miss our picnic days,
Our Sunday walks after *Moruti* Nkomo's preaching about adultery
yet he kisses Dipuo late after Sermon.
I have been learning how to iron these days;
I will help you with cooking, I can make nice fat cakes now . . . you know! –
You will love them.

My love, it's only three weeks away.
I will kiss you like tomorrow never comes.
I hope you get this letter on time.

I LOVE YOU from this life and the next.

From

THABO

Tshediso Seroki

'*Tsela ya sefapano*': Sesotho expression meaning way of the cross, normally read by Roman Catholic, ***Moruti:*** Sesotho/Sepedi/Setswana meaning Priest

A NEST UPON AN ALMOND TREE

Up an almond tree were crows in a *nest,*
For days we'd watched them build it to their best.

This nest was artistic; it had little twigs and bits of old *rags,*
Little twigs from maidenhair trees and old rags from old battered bags.

My friends and I, one day thought of killing these *birds* –
To the dazed, muttering inferences of words,

We tried as they flew away; we did lotsa shooting *then,*
But we never took shots whilst they were still in their den.

Oh No, – my dear, we did not eat the *crows,*
We just had just time to hunt while herding the cows!

The parent crow was completely laden with *greed,*
In the bush we oftentimes witnessed its deed;

We saw some nuts it purloined from the fields and *hidden,*
It never cared whether the farmer was ill or bedridden.

We could've sommer killed it cos it's a *thief,*
But its hue (black), frightening –we'd come to grief.

And it felt rather safer for us to leave it *alone,*
Especially that we dwelled on our Pat Malone;

I know not what urged us want to kill them by the tree in the *sun,*
Perchance it was because we thought it could be a lotta fun;

In essence they just made us catch feelings to make us *scared,*
Perhaps just to conserve their artistic nest lingering stared.

Up an almond tree were crows in their *nest*,
For days I'd watched the mates build it to the best.

Choene Semenya

Den: an animal's lair; **purloined**: stole; **bedridden**: unable to get out of bed because of sickness or oldness; **hue**: colour; **Pat Malone**: alone; **lotta**: lot of

STREET LIGHTS BURNT THE MOTH

Mother, I stand here next to
pavement with a face wearing empty
promises of tomorrow. I sniffed
white lines for my black lies; I can
no longer smell the coffee. To me
living in the light is no longer a
metaphor.

Prayers exit my bleeding spirit in
search for state of salvation. Many
times this concrete next to street
lights look like a mouse trap, the
truth stays awake like insomnia
when I seek for a nap.

In relation to relationships I have
taken refuge on falling tides for
when morning comes the sea has
spit me out in the cold and waiting
for another Fix.

How do I fix this?

Father, if brokenness is Hereditary I
inherited your wounds. I'm trying to
fit where you walked but your steps
are greater for me to fit. I know I'm
your child mother, for I no longer
wait for the fat lady to sing. I write
for her songs of my sadness. She
adopted my odes as my lamenting
chorus.

'Tis cold here, and sun burns where
wings ought to grow; brother I
have seen many lives fading into
addictions, and it's on the narrow
corridors of our ceramic hearts
where we seek passage to freedom,
and every squeeze squash bones.
HERE I stand, ribs torn, lungs
collecting fainting breaths body
temperature dropping like standards
of morality.

Here lights are like beacons of hope.
It's dark to go back home – mother
put me in your prayers tonight as it
is darker where I'm heading.

Tshediso Seroki

ADIEU GRANDPA, ADIEU!

Adieu Grandpa, adieu as you transit with death!
Oh, therefore we lament, as we sadly lay you to rest.
Bon voyage Grandpa, bon voyage, as away sail your breath;
You were slain by your years, but you fulfilled your quest.
Your life on earth, a blessing to multitudes more,
Oh Grandpa, can you believe it?
Your demise from life, of course, 'twas a nature's roar –
But true this, I cannot withstand it!
Neither crystals of gold nor a diamond, but indelible a memory you left,
Upon your pilgrim towards the pearly gate:

Allow us to honour you,
Allow us to mourn you –
O, in terms of love,
Permit us all to miss you!

I say, not vanity nor conceit, but of your wisdom we are bereft;
You breathed your last, of course that was fate,
Not a million-million words of sighs and tears can bring you back;
We shall lay you, O, as in memory of you my soul sings
Sad hymns that shall heal your children and keep them on track –
Rejoice, from your eternal sleep, in the state kindly shared with kings!

Choene Semenya

Adieu: French for goodbye, bon voyage has the corresponding meaning;
transit: travel away; **indelible**: unforgettable; **pilgrim**: a journey to a holy
place

BEHIND CLOSED DOORS

Her face touched the ground of his hard palms;
blue eyes saw the memoirs of fading charms flashing in his strong arms.

His smile keeps changing pattern like rubric cubes,
chest for Pandora's Box beats failing love tubes.

Receiving end always leave the mess
Morning comes, face decorated in bruises.

Smiles shaded behind make up to try fix the cosmos
that got swallowed by the wormhole.

Morning bids farewell to a happy homes.
Walls are crumbling; painting is shedding off its light.

Tshediso Seroki

THE NIGHT

I love the night.
The consolation of the night, the shining of the moon,
The dissipating of bracing twilights post late afternoon,
The singing of birds, the effulgence of stars,
The sound of fair winds rustling the grass,
The blow of the breeze, the glister of a moon shining fair,
The quietude of a luminous plate floating in the air,
The peace unsullied by the dirt, the teasing of the mind,
The dancing of the moon to the gentle night wind,
The tsau! tsau! of stars, the moon hungry again,
The way of the night with a strange sound of rain –
Flourishes wee tares all that might.
I love the night.

Choene Semenya

Consolation: comfort; **bracing**: fresh and invigorating; **effulgence**: shiny
state; **breeze**: a gentle wind; **glister**: glow, shining; **quietude**: state of total
quietness; **luminous**: bright, glowing; **unsullied**: unspoiled

IN THE MOMENT

Something in the stars savoured taste of broken hearts,
Crumbling homes, shattering bones.
In deep of falling forever words are monuments
to remember.

Something in the flowing rivers keeps codes of
hidden tongues spoken by elders.
Ships board waves of mysterious frequencies;
Air dense enough to give life.

Something in breaking waters of emerging dawn,
let go of your burdens they unmount reason out of your temple.
Behold your breath.

Tshediso Seroki

O WINTER!

O winter, winter, yes winter, you are so cold.
I tell you what I know and not what I been told.

O winter, winter, in your presence trees shrink,
Oh I'm so cold —I can't breathe, I can't think.

O winter, winter, why is but your night so long?
Birds no longer put me to sleep with their melodious song.

Why are you so chilly, why are you so dark?
Your darkness is like the throat of a shark.

O winter, winter, to where have you taken the moon?
Please say to me it will come back soon.

Your coldness makes me ill with flu and fever,
When you're gone, I just wish you'd be gone forever.

O winter, winter, where have you been hiding in summer;
When mom took me to school to learn language grammar?

You make me scared, winter, as much as you make me sad.
You possess evil – you disgust me, you really make me mad.

You always make it hard for me to wake up in the morning;
And I'll go shower half asleep, the whole day I'll be yawning.

Choene Semenya

HIS FADING WHISPER

He kneels on the shores hoping for the dirt beneath his feet to be washed,
He picked pieces of his remaining ego as broken shells.
Chest heavy to hold inhalations, guilt grabbed his throat he choked,
He shed off his skin in search for the matching skeleton.

He found oversized empty heart he gazed up in the air for a way out,
His voice coarse enough to make a loud noise.
He sang grace from regret filled lips draping his monologue,
From answers questioning his whereabouts to
Questions answering his could have been.

He looks for a way out and found God in his darkness.
He bows his head as if asking gravity about his loneliness.
Grace!!

Tshediso Soroki

TREES

What is this spring if, laden with grief,
I have a wish to see trees coming into leaf

And their foliage nourishing, beginning afresh –
And being as soft as the touch of Zaldania's flesh;

And their verdance gleaming in the sun,
Where children can hide and seek and have fun.

A wish to lie beneath the trees and watch the stars,
At night when breeze sways humbly the grass;

And the boughs of trees rustling in the cold,
Like something poetic almost being told.

A wish to hear jovial birds chirping in trees during the day –
To relish their melodies and their vernal songs and be gay;

A wish to lo and behold with a smile, trees growing high,
Come new season, they seem to say with a beseeching sigh;

And wash away these shriveled leaves again,
So we can blossom new lease of grain –

And help recover the branches that were cut into wood,
By these people who reside in the neighbourhood;

A wish to sit and watch the trees dance,
To fulfill my leisure whilst I enjoy their glance.

And sing a jolly song as I watch them shake,
Hence slumber in their shadow and tarry to wake;

Just like they once died and then began anew,
I also wish that if I die I come back too.

O dreadful this spring if, laden with grief,
I have a wish to see the trees coming into leaf.

Choene Semenya

Verdance: greenness, state of being fresh and green; **beseeching**: asking earnestly, requesting; **jovial**: cheerful; **relish**: enjoy; **vernal**: of spring, connected with spring; **gay**: thrilled, happy; **tarry**: delay, take your time

KOOVUKIE RIVER

It was a fair river —narrow, lugging, etc.
Its flow, like the tidewater, was strong,
But it didn't roar. Its sight, life-giving
Was ripping —the flow that sounded like a song,
In buckets of rain.

And all the people praised it.

Its days were a gob of wonderments. It flowed off
Hills, rose up and down coarse terrains, swished
Squillion river loads at a time, went down with pride;
Flooding —it was jus' a valour happenstance —
In buckets of rain.

And all the people praised it.

But was the flow of its own? Yes, but never
The peril. Those fishermen that fished at the river bank
Were brave men. How was the Koovukie River then?
In full spate. Water whirling as in a tank —
its zephyr, refreshing, everyone doted upon it;
In buckets of rain.

And all the people praised it.

Months later, severe drought struck the terrain;
Little or no rain, zilch at all, sprinkled the territory.
All flowers and roses at its riverside withered dead —
Its mouth ran completely dry. Now its sight, eyesore!
Aquatic creatures in it: fishes, crabs, frogs, etc.
Went on a deathly hibernation;
Two years elapsed, 'twas wholly arid; little poor river
ultimately had nothing to proffer,
In fear of drought, gasping for rain.

Rain did not fall –
It was then devoid of breeze and pizzazz,
In absence of rain.

And all the people deserted it.

Choene Semenya

Lugging: pulling heavy objects; **ripping**: wonderful; **squillion**: a large number; **valour happenstance**: brave chance; **doted upon it**: loved it; **hibernation**: a sleep-like state that happens for a long time; **arid**: dry; **proffer**: offer; **devoid of**: completely lacking in

ON THE OTHER SIDE

On the other side of the grave sits weary spirits
of worn out Elders,

Young spirits descend due to circumstances.
Prayers failing
Others refuse their calling,
On the other side of crimes
Dark tapes seal witnesses with guilt –
Another victim in pool of blood,
these streets we have built.
Dreams die before they find shape,
On the other side of the sea, shores
Still mourn our
Whitewashed brains.

Tshediso Seroki

WEALTHY BLOKE

He wasn't rich but stinking wealthy.
He was always on everybody's lips –
His voice was heard and praised;
His attire, of exorbitant pomposity, was ritzy;
And never fair, vibrant vinos he dearly adored.

He loved and led life of la dolce vita –
His amour proper was of irksome imperiousness,
His cars, of pricey standard, were fascinating;
And never cared, beggars sprawling at the corners of the streets
He stared like imps.

He travelled a lot:
Colombia, USA, London, Addis Ababa, Japan, etc.
He spoke eighteen languages at a time,
But just a smattering of Chinese;
His accent, like that of the US, was embellished
And girls he changed like cheap toys.

Few years later,
Irremediable ailment caught up with him;
And he was taken to the most expensive hospice in the country.
He was bedridden:
He couldn't walk, he couldn't talk or smile or blink –
Yet nobody ever went see him in hospice.

Days went with him getting from worse to worst,
Until he sank into a coma.
Media gobbled his condition like famished vultures –
His gloomy story appeared all over the papers,
Was heard in the news of radio,
And was seen on television.

He couldn't work anymore, and his luxury faded:
Failed to maintain his life, failed to pay the bills;

And hence later on, the secret of his heavy illnesses was revealed –
That's when we all learnt that he had:
HIV/AIDS, GONORRHOEA, SYPHILIS and late stage
SARCOMIC PROSTATE CANCER;
Several horrendous conditions that reminds everyone
that they are still human, however rich they are.
Lamentably, a few days later his heart stopped going abeat –
And his breath was last and breathless,
And sadly, he died.

And guess what:
No one went to his burial.

Choene Semenya

Wealthy: very rich; **exorbitant pomposity**: intending to impress because it is expensive; **ritzy**: fashionable; **vinos**: wines; **la dolce vita**: a Latin phrase meaning an expensive life without worry; **irksome imperiousness**: irritating expectance of unquestioning obedience; **imps**: small devils; **smattering**: a slight knowledge of something; **embellished**: decorated; **irremediable**: not curable; **hospice**: a hospital of the seriously ill; **horrendous**: horrible

LET'S SPEAK IN TONGUES

We have been strangers.
Our lips forgot how to sing together after the baby is born.

We have been strangers to ancient
Drums calling from far ends of nearby villages;
Now communities look away from each other –
Sons and daughters burn to ashes as now every man is
for Himself.

Bon-fires no longer hold stories of heroes
Truth dressed and disguised as hate.
Let's dust off the dirt on our lips and
sing praises for each other's triumph.

Let's form a circle of life and
relearn how to love
our neighbours.

Camagu!!

Tshediso Seroki

Camagu: appreciation token for ancestors normally during ceremonies
after an elder spoke (Xhosa tribe)

WISH OF THE SLACKER

Stars are shining in the sky,
Larks are singing in the rain,
And the waters are tremulous
In the cold.

The flooding rivers go on flowing,
And the coquettish girls go on flirting
But I'm longing, simply longing
For this rain to awash this
my pluviophile self.
When I am outside, feeling a lot better,

When I am in the house no longer,
When raining times and days all fade,
If there is shining in the sky,
If larks are singing in the rain no longer,
If waters are tremulous,
If the rain is dead, down and dusted,
I'll be out to mourn the rain.

Choene Semenya

Slacker: a lazy person; **tremulous**: shaking; quaky; **coquettish**: flirty;
pluviophile: a lover of rain

FROM *Biting the dust*

I, not a thing:
I wish I see it again
Life is too short and ceases
When you least expect it
It that luves me wants to
Waste me
Cos it luves me with a
Hateful luve –
Luve, possessed by hate
Comes from the depth of
Hell,
From a hideous side of
God's infamy
And I know; I am jus' a
Flowing rivulet –
A mirage of nothingness
The vultures are cumin' to
Get me
O Perfect!
But I won't let them put me
In a straitjacket, in a coffin
Nae sirree!
I will live like
I used to live ere
Free!
But to bite the dust:
Perchance to embark on a
Pilgrimage,
May I die – but die painlessly!

Choene Semenya

Hideous: extremely unpleasant; **Infamy**: evil behavior; an evil act; **rivulet**:
a small river; a small stream of water; **pilgrimage**: a journey to a holy place

TO THOSE WHO. . .

Where there is smoke, fire awaits to blossom into flames;
Fingers seeking comfort in the arms our crippled crimson tides,
Stories coiled within cow hides,
Tell tales of girls losing their innocence like rose petals.
Into the dark we learn how to drink our spirits out of bottles of vodka,
We see reality from perspective of aborted souls
We never manifest to who we are.

Walls of broken hearts catching fire,
For ribs are made of logs dry enough for bonfire.
Pathway to life is a narrow corridor of dreams,
Keeping grudge burdens the chest.
Closet a dungeon of haunting regrets.

Knees and hands on beggars' position, prayers for this dying season,
To those who are in search are still looking, and nothing seems clearer.
Behold your visions and see them take shape
Into what your faith decorates.

Tshediso Seroki

YOU LOVED ME

You fell in love with me when we first met,
Sighing from where you stood, nigh the wall;
Then, you belle, who longs kissing lips wet:
I loved you too with the breath, smiles and tears of all
My life!
Now say I'm broke, say I'm lazy,
Say that there's nothing left 'twixt you and me,
Say I'm jejune, haply even crazy,
But forget not to enthuse that you once loved me.

Choene Semenya

Belle: the most beautiful girl in a particular place, **jejune**: boring, dull;
enthuse: say enthusiastically

REDRAW ME

Redraw me back in time where clocks were Titans guarding the front of forever, Walls of our hearts shepherds to astray heartbeats leading them to empty love.

Reshape my contours, and align me back to labyrinth of my elders' covenant. Gravity, let go of my weight, and let my bones levitate.

My mother's strings of celo moving within my father's guitar base, I, the music born to life – a high note of ancient beauty of forever; Prithee, redraw me!

Tshediso Seroki

Titans: giants; **astray**: off the path; **contours:** outlines; **labyrinth:** complexity; **prithee**: please (exclamation used to indicate a polite request)

A GOODBYE KISS

I kissed my beloved Joyce at the shallow waters of the sea
At sundown after a scorching day of summer's sun
'Neath the purely dark cumulonimbus that scudded in the hazy sky
In the sprinkles of rain that washed the lovelorn day off me
On the beach witnessed by the inquisitive starfishes and crabs
Over the velvety beach sand that tickled pink
the underside skin of my feet
Nigh the lazy ebb and flow of the tidewater that jinxed perhaps me

She then voyaged with the Titanic that went evanescent
In the rising waves of the sea (standing on the prow of the ship)
Thereby the quay stood I ergo,
And gazed forlornly over the twilit space of a reproachful atmosphere
As the zonked out sun sunk deep down the bottomless nature
Of the earth to roost;
Long enough 'til I knew it kissed the bowels of its sightless end –
That is when I perceived the transitory nature of luve,
Nevertheless, the goodbye kiss she had given me
Haunts me forevermore without a comma or a semicolon.

Choene Semenya

Scorching: extremely hot; **velvety**: pleasantly smooth and soft; **tidewater**: the flow of water that happens as the sea rises and falls, often at an area of land near the coast; **jinxed**: brought bad luck; **voyaged**: travelled in a ship over a long distance; **Titanic**: the most largest ship; **evanescent**: disappearing quickly from sight; **zonked out**: extremely tired; **roost**: rest; **transitory**: fleeting; temporary

I WILL KILL

With charms of stars I will kill the darkness.
With rainbow of charms I will kill storms across your face.
With silence I will kill ignorance until my speech
improves understanding.

These are specks of dust in the eyes of my people,
There is no bliss in ignorance.
Symphonies of dust in hiding will kill western airs we breathe.
I will kill insecurities; bury them in shallow grave –
These skeletons in closest keeps knocking doors
like poltergeist.

With my hands hanging in the air I will battle spirit of hate
To change our fate;
I will battle the angel of death in the Middle East,
Where blood of the innocent spill more than ruins of war scattered.
I will kill angel of death for life is precious than oil spills;
With drums and chants I will interpret ancestral songs back to life
Then I will lose western biblical ways.

With incense burns I will ash down the,
What is not and rebuild what is.
With sorghum beer spills I will ask for calabashes
to hold waters as birth waits.

I will break walls, create new paths, I will kill.
Seeing is believing, yet sight disregarded by those who inherit the eyes,
Lesson learnt without blood soon forgotten –
Beauty lies in the eyes, beholder doesn't see where steps are misleading.
One wise man said:

'Dismember your radar if you want to arrive.'
Spirit particle depletes, fingerprints recognise texture of truth.
Unwind the cycle in windmills; winds know where dust can rest.
Relevance over gluttony, –

Who bites more than they chew
When souls can't remember where sight lost sense?
Remember to see,
Remember to seek,
Remember to seek and see,
Remember why you see!

Tshediso Seroki

THE LIZARD

I was but only six years old,
When I first espied a lizard in the cold.
From where it reposed, just 'neath the roof on the wall,
Well-nigh comatose, it felt the warmth not at all –
It was quaking, it was perished, it was pale I dare say...
Shivering in the arctic morn I saw it attempt to move away,

But it could not, since its blood was nigh a pang of rime;
Vainly it squirmed restlessly, timeously with a tick of time.
From the bowels of its heart I knew it sought the shining sun;
Barefaced – and what it felt at that jiffy I still can't tell for one.
And the only parts it usually uses when it crawls
Every time it willed to move was always its paws.

Then it showed a look on its face, of intolerable gloom
(Too cowing for the lizard to bear holding onto that room)
And bang! –it proceeded a bit, fretfully though, and wrung a tear.
O poor lizard, just a mite that loved the sun so near and dear.
Typical of reptiles; its rough skin awful and somewhat strange –
Things about reptiles: cold-blooded, meek, never one shall change.

And then I gasped; it glared at me with its minute eyes hardly open to
behold;
As if it thought I were the one who effaced the sun and brought upon the
cold.
That morning, in my tender age, was when I first espied a lizard in the
cold so clear,
And ever since that parky forenoon, either warm or cold, I see a lizard
every year.

Choene Semenya

'neath: beneath; **comatose:** in a coma; **arctic:** extremely cold; **pang:** large amount; **rime:** frost; **squirmed:** wriggled; **barefaced:** undisguised, open; **gloom:** unhappiness; **cowing:** threatening; **proceeded:** moved; **wrung a tear:** cried; **mite:** tiny creature; **minute:** tiny **effaced:** removed, made disappear; **parky forenoon:** chilly morning

SPIRITUAL SONNETS (PSALM 1)

I died.

Coffin of a body carrying much weight,
Bones heavier as my light, wait!

No, I died; I saw light at the end of the tunnel,
My coffin made in form of mysterious labyrinth,
As I tried to be a better man it changed its shape,
Paradigm shift has never looked so unclear.

I died.

Afraid to be alone in the dark with poison
Calabash broke like first dawn, tears raided my tomb;
The door opened promised land,
Like a young angel who traded his halo
For a misused fabrics of trust.

I died.

There are scars beneath my skin,
There is no hope within my reach,
Life and meaning seeming to be farfetched.

I died.

The door opened in front of me and I saw my life
flashing in spectrum dying memories,
Maybe it was me bidding me farewell.
Knees finished from praying,
War lost, chest for warzone, heartbeat for bombs –
Skeletons in my closet dressed with my peeling skin,

If death is deep then my sockets rather be hand
Full of minerals. I died not to be born again,
But to bury the yet to be born again inconceivable pain.

I died.

Tshediso Seroki

FATE YOU ARE INSANE!

Fate you are insane! Fate you are insane!
Do not fate on my life ever again –
Wherefore is it that you only excommunicate,
Are you not afraid of grudges and hate?

Fate you are insane! Fate you are insane!
You seem obsessed with curse and pain –
Whence comes your arrogance and empty pride,
And from your malice how can my visage hide?

Fate you are insane! Fate you are insane!
Our friendship has failed like winter rain –
Wherein do sit your fear and your dread,
Because mercy in your heart is a word dead?

Fate you are insane! Fate you are insane!
Death is my fear, but you are my main –
To that you fate, to that eternally I weep,
For you fated my father to his eternal sleep.

Fate you are insane! Fate you are insane!
From you I've so much to lose but less to gain –
You looked like a gentleman, from soul to crown,
But you've proven yourself to be a creepy clown.

Fate you are insane! Fate you are insane!
You are wicked –you distort my brain –
As I endeavour to understand you and all,
And you let love, joy, peace, to chaos fall.

O fate, deranged how can you be,
Or should I wait for more to see?
Shall your providence does my soul divide,
And leave me, oh fate, with a wounded pride?

And forever distinguish me from delight,
Just because I blame you, 'FATE' every night?
Fate you are insane, most than a viral strain;
I reiterate, you are I-N-S-A-N-E –insane!

Choene Semenya

BURY ME WITH A PEN

For where I'm going there is a promise land,
Not tears and pain given first hand.
There truth lies naked than sacred tombs,
Where I stand I've seen many graves from wounded wombs.
Looking back at farmlands of my forefathers,
I see their spirits looking for prodigal sons lost in
the concrete jungle.

Mother cry not, for I have served a purpose,
With pen in my coffin I will write your tears on walls of eternity,
Brother help father to carry the cross on his shoulders like
angels with their shining halos.

Tell my sons and daughters to harness their dreams with prayer.
I will write their names at the womb of dawn when it breaks;
Its first water, sun born tattoos as ways to follow light,
I will reshape destiny of my beloved.

Mother, your tears will be scattered across the cosmos like stars.
I met my elders forming circle of life,
Life after death is carved on my bones.
I will scribe love on palm prints of rain drops
For when it rains my soul touches my kind.

Bury me with a pen.
With ink I will rewrite myself
Like phoenix teaching flames to live,
Eternity with lie beyond infinity.

My pen will carry our burdens to the gods,
They will know of death where black lives live.
With all the might of a pen, frequencies will birth
Music from sad smiles of aborted infants.

I will keep writing hymns for my old age to remind
Youth of wrinkles wrapped in stories untold.
Mummify my skin with layers of QURAN,
I will learn how to fly mats like Alladin.

I will pick a fight with Titans so I bleed spiritually;
Bury me with a pen to draft my footprints on sands of time –
Remember me,
I will write songs to dying winds to resurrect tornadoes
and typhoons. I will draw names of forgotten Kings,
To change the spirit of things.

Therefore, bury me with a pen.

Tshediso Seroki

Quran: is the central religious text of Islam, which Muslims believe to be
a revelation from God (Allah)

THE ABANDONED ADOLESCENT

My grandmother told me my mother left me when I was young,
But she said my father she never knew –
Though I bet auntie knew something
About both my parents and everything,
Because she once said: 'My nephew,
I feel for you but I'm afraid I can't help you find he and she here among
So many selfish men and women who deliberately abandoned their kids.'
Yet the ignoble rumours kept on waving to my ears –
Rumours that said my father was a ladies' man,
Like me; he was a studmuffin back then,
A handsome man who had no worries and no fears
About what other people said about him on the streets.
But no one wants to tell me what happened 'twixt my mother and him;
What made both of them to desert me –
If or whether I was an element of surprise,
Because the merit of my identity is full of lies.
This man claims to be my father, who is he?
Auntie says it's true and that his sobriquet is Cass, his name Jim.
I know not what to believe for I thought my father was dead,
But there is something I will never forget –
Because the soothsayer foretold it all
Long time ago when I was still small;
He said my father would one day return and let
Me know everything. Pity he came caring only a brown bread;
But still, he is my father. O dear Ma, where are you?
My father has returned whence he had come –
I was love-struck and I made a lady pregnant,
And I don't know who to turn to for everyone is distant;
O come home Ma, wherever you are, just come home.
I have accepted my father as he is and surely I'll accept you too.
Mother please, hear me out, wherever you are I know you're certainly
gloomed.
But think of me, a precious thing you left behind –
A concerned adolescent who can never be proud
Of who he is when he's confused with his identity all about;

Don't tell me that coming back to your son has never crossed your mind,
Because I am yours, and what matters is that my future be not I'm doomed.

Choene Semenya

Ignoble: dirty, disgracing, dishonourable; **studmuffin:** a man who is considered sexually attractive; **merit:** point, aspects of something; **sobriquet:** nickname; **soothsayer:** a person who is believed to be able to tell what will happen in the future, prophet; **gloomed:** sad and embarrassed

FORGIVE ME

Snowflakes build a snow man for summer holds a promise for snowman
to melt;
I promise to follow where my heart leads no matter the fears I have felt.
Not to mention my heart beats, they have tendency of moving like angry
floods,
Forgive my flaws to drag you into my demented world,
At least in you I saw the paradise that evermore but had me hoping.
Heaven on earth I saw in your eyes,
Chest hiding where the truth lies.
Smile! Your smile a space ship to make me go and
Come back from the hour glass;

Forgive me.

My heart is a retard, yet for you I have fallen so hard.
Forgive my heart for loving your heart this deep;
Forgive me for bringing you this magnitude of temptation
As form of happiness.
I profusely apologise. I'm not perfect, and I'm far from it –
My steps keep with the movement of the tortoise,
My lips have been spilling your name through like the hour glass,
Crystal for crystal, I keep my thirst open because
I frankly cannot get enough; my heart just wants more.

Forgive me.

Wars on knees at times signifies submission,
I submitted my anchors to your center.
Every prayer, for my collapsed lung walls, is drawn for you.
Now please forgive me. If my wrongs were the only thing left,
Then you'd have the right to call me tin man – empty chest no heart.
Yet I can swallow my pride for you to be the lioness.

On tanzanite crystals your name I will engrave on my tomorrows,
Lest I grant audience to your unsaid sorrows.
I will breath to enclose you in the lining of my lungs.

Forgive me.

Tshediso Seroki

LINDSAY LAIS

Lindsay Lais was an attractive lassie who feared for her life;
Whose life was appalling that she'd always carried a knife –
Everywhere she went she was jumpy and full of fright,
And she would never walk in the eve, in the fading light.
She was friends with nobody; never could she share her anguish,
Nor could she tell anyone of her pain and fear or her inherent wish.
It was one dewy morning when I first saw her cry –a rare phenomenon;
In fact, even when she was upset or hurt she never wept till that morn:
And the dreaded tears from her eyes, dropping like spring dew –
It was surrealistic, for those who could make her weep were very few.
And surprisingly, her tears were not full of sadness but full of empty joy,
Just because she had lost her beau and then met another boy.
And now all her fears have gone AWOL, like a winter sun –
Ever since she had met the new guy who has a gun.

Choene Semenya

Lassie: girl; **appalling**: very unpleasant, terrible; **anguish**: torment, mental
suffering or unhappiness; **inherent**: dearest, deep-rooted; **phenomenon**:
occurrence; **surrealistic**: very strange, like a dream; **beau**: boyfriend

CIRCUMSTANCES MADE ME WHO I AM

Circumstances made me who I am.
Born from discarded past where gun shots still
Holds memories of fallen heroes;
Shebeens school more junkies and drunkards –
Jail palisades still hold dying dreams of my kind.

The remains of decomposing energies
still hold tunes composing these energies,
On my knees waiting for grace to face
skins of my melancholy.

My kind waging wars for land where privileges always white,
but in truth my kind always lose the fight.
Circumstances made me who I am.
Congregations made to swallow petrol to fuel the holy fire,
My kind exploited in search for miracles over night,
It's them told to eat snakes to heal the curse of Cain
Due to the idea of sweat glands keeping a break for miracles
to knock heaven's door, when sisters accept fire and roll on the floor.

Circumstances made me who I am.

Weekend specials young infant died from cross infection,
Mothers weep their still born as a result,
This education, dedication to create bunch of unemployed graduates,
Look at the crime rate, it's on the rise due to unemployment
roaming the dusty streets.
First time I met god was when my cocaine lines wrote heaven is for real.

Circumstances made me who I am.

Mountain tops breed gangsters not initiates,
streets more hostile than battle grounds;
everywhere over the weekend a tent fits more bodies to mourn their own,
Survival of the fittest is the only goal.

Circumstances made me who I am.

Tshediso Seroki

GRUMPY SUCCESSFUL WOMAN

There cries a woman who feels unloved and forlorn,
Just because what she loved was hurt and gone;
This woman always wanted things to go her way –
And her attitude always drove her loved ones away.
She is bossy, egotistical and a little bit too proud,
She has money, fame and her character a bit too loud;
She used to think everything revolved around her,
And now all she can ever say is that life is not fair.
From where can she get solace when what she loved she lost?
Yet she bargains with God and prays with her fingers crossed –
To be successful with money and all, but leading a loveless life,
Renders her grumpy and amputates her soul with a lovelorn knife;
O this woman, whether loved or not, she used to pretend never to care,
But now that she needs that love, that love is no longer there.

Choene Semenya

THE HOUSE WE BUILT

Red riding hood, for blood is thicker than water when everything ALTERS.
EGO changes stages with its growth, yet in the house we built
Mats hold on the dirt we keep under carpets hoping things to come to
place. Hearts on Richter scale when chest are shaken by angry beats,
This house we built on quick sand keep sinking in;
Our wardrobes dress skeletons in closets.
Family secrets hanging on doormats where everyone
who comes for a visit sees how broken the foundation we lay on is.

Family gatherings, a place to open old wounds,
Christmas lunches to find way to lick debris from broken blue prints;
Envy a Christmas charol. Snowmen built from old grudges documented on
Ever correct wealthy uncle –This house we built;
Smiles and fake grins to paint window frames,
When jealousy jets to set seats on fire, who burns first?
We dine with knives under our tables,
Black sheep for a sacrifice when throats are slit,
Who cries for graves when house has forgotten names?

This house we built is a tomb where souls rest to lay fears to rest where that
Unemployed uncle becomes everyone's burden;
See, family tree is at stake.
This house we built from shattered pieces of broken cups.
Children – the only pieces finding peace when night falls
for they don't know better.
This is the house we built; from dust we cement grudges on top of each
other like we stack monarchies from demolished empires.
This is the house we built from scratches leaving marks to mark
Where scars are buried.
See, no family is perfect.

Tshediso Seroki

Charol: From Latinoamérica meaning tray;

THE SMILE

Joyce asked me out to a likeable beach
Ruth asked me out to the lurid movies
Elizabeth to the frolicsome dance festival
Goodness to the magical Piccadilly circus
But Mokgadi none but smiled at me:
And nooit asked me out at all.

Joyce and I kissed on the quayside
Ruth and I at the theater's front seats
Elizabeth and I in the flooding crowd
Goodness and I only hugged backstage
Though Mokgadi kissed me never –
She jus' smiled at me
And the smile on her visage
Torments me every so oft,
Day in and day out!

Choene Semenya

Lurid: horrifying; **nooit**: from Afrikaans meaning never; **Piccadilly Circus**: used to describe a place full of people

GIVE ME A NAME

My name is discarded due to premature destinies,
Abortion still birth more soldiers in the afterlife
my name awaits to be named.
Abducted in pamper of night to be called refugee in foreign land.
See, there are names given to even scores of dismantled past,
A girl named a prostitute was only a daughter of a single mother.
No mother waits to hear her daughter's passing –
It hurts when news hit the eardrums.
Call me a statistic, anything you want but not yet son of the soil.

Name me a soldier carrying guns to bury sons.
See, they made me this name,
See, with this name comes discrepancies;
I killed a man waiting for his son to return from war –the man was my
father.
I killed my father to inherit his name.
Call me anything from this circumstance.
My palms were forced to be the midwife to pull the fetus from mother's
womb;
I have buried my brothers hands full of dirtied soil stained with blood.
See, innocent children always lose their mark due to unfavourable
predicaments.

To gain a name of a hero I became a villain in my village.
Yet still I don't have a name.
Seeing my sisters falling like dominoes breaks my heart
like skulls smashed against hard walls of my ego.
I have seen legs spread on dirty sheets of adultery
yet my name a flame that burnt the bridges,
Call me a hero in the art of falling tears.

I know not my name for these street corners are smeared with my fears.
I saw skins of bisons wrapped around necks of mortal man,
such burden heavier than guilt.
Rivers ululate in their rhythm in search for lost melodies.

No one heard gunshots when bodies bore a relentless onslaught,
Bags for caskets to lead names six feet,
Tombs to be on chest of dead bodies.
Dream!!!

My name is NO MERCY!
I killed my bloodlines to be named a desert of lost souls.
Name me anything, anything but not Black.

Tshediso Seroki

LUCIFER

He is as dangerous the man, like no other man I've ever met –
His heart is black though his face is pally;
He's friendly –that shows so little of him.
And thus does the fact that he has a cheerful smile.
But let me tell you something, my sweet,
His smile is deceiving; his friendliness is perilous.
Even though he speaks so softly,
Whenever he speaks he barely pauses,
With his big round eyes sweeping around and about you,
straining to circumvent the righteousness of your insight;
Because he's trying to hide the last icy-cold wrongs of
     His heinous life.
He talks a lot but never does he speak loud his thoughts –
He's doggedly single-minded,
And the ugly thoughts he thinks he never rethinks.
He's like a snake in your garden, rattling under
     Your favourite flora –as green as hue green is pure;
Waiting for you to lose focus; Perhaps to misstep.
He's but a friend but an arch foe;
He never laughs with you, he laughs at you;
And he has no ruth for those who tell the truth –
He's here to steal, to kill and to destroy, those who
     Know no prayer.
He is psychotic I dare say; and I like to add
That when he sees you perhaps in church, praying,
     Regardless of your belief –
He goes utterly ballistic; his heart grows indefinitely detestable,
And jealousy is the only dominant sentiment simmering within him;
For he knows he cannot influence you, or steal from you, or kill you
     Nor can he destroy you –and believe you me,
My sweet, that's his greatest worry.
He's surreptitiously playing a tireless game to purloin
     Your dearest life: To defile you –
To fulfill the infinity of his contempt and the eternity
     Of his jealousy; for his anger never ceases nor his soul do rest,

Until he gets precisely what he wants:
Convincing you to confuse you, to not take a route less voyaged by.
He's a devil, a calculating slayer, enemy of success, a fearless moron.
Yes, his thoughts are worse, but his demeanour is worst;
That no despicable deed to him is ever unorthodox;
But methinks with time you'll live and with time you'll learn'
Which route is key to take for prosperity of your subsistence –
Even you who do not take my poem to heart,
    I assure you, you're dead alive not to notice his unspeakable intentions –
So I advise you, be circumspect whenever you're about him,
    My sweet.

Choene Semenya

Pally: friendly; **circumvent**: avoid, dodge; **heinous**: wicked, terrible, shocking; **doggedly**: tenaciously, determinedly; **he's but a friend but an arch foe**: he's not a friend, he is a main enemy whereas he pretends to be a friend; **psychotic**: crazy; **ballistic**: became very angry; **surreptitiously**: secretly; **voyaged**: travelled; **purloin**: steal; **demeanour**: behaviour; **unorthodox**: unacceptable; **subsistence**: existence; **circumspect**: cautious

THOSE

Those

Scars are the only language these graves speak.
Those who died with mouths closed still scream with clench fist.
What do I tell those who are yet to be born?
What do I tell them when they ask me about LANDS OF FOREFATHERS?

Those

Shady handshakes and hollow smiles still steal moments of my words with
Silence. Syllables tend to miss more I love yous and warm embraces.

Those

Scars beneath shades of your thousand faces,
Wait! What about those skeletons in your closet?

Tshediso Seroki

DRUG ADDICT

I first saw him sitting ramblingly in the sweltering sun,
His eyes were red and his lips were cracked and dry –
He had not even seen me, nor did he hear me pass by;
'Could've seen how young he was, claiming to have fun;
He smelt of marijuana a reek that failed the flies
That tend to buzz all day long under blue summer skies.

And I saw him sprawling again in the thrashing cold,
Rolling Nyaope in a cut newspaper wrapping a fold;
As I passed near him, where the road did bend –
I realized it wasn't just Nyaope, but a commingling blend.
He smelt of marijuana a reek that failed the flies
That tend to buzz all day long under blue summer skies.

And on the next morrow when I went to buy a bread,
I saw him leaning against an abandoned yard's fence,
I pitied him; as if he didn't know the risks of smoking –hence,
The drugs feebled him, he fell and had lain as if he was dead;
He smelt of marijuana a reek that failed the flies
That tend to buzz all day long under blue summer skies.

And I saw him the other day, smoking heavily alone,
With his eyes closed, sitting upon the base of a stone.
He looked untidy and parched, hungry and lost –
Wearing a moth-eaten shirt that was faded brown almost;
He smelt of marijuana a reek that failed the flies
That tend to buzz all day long under blue summer skies.

And I saw him another day, he was at the same place;
He was puffing and blowing out a thick dark smoke
That wasted the atmospheric fresh air – O poor oke!
Saliva was breaking limply from his lips, from a mouth of his face;
He smelt of marijuana a reek that failed the flies
That tend to buzz all day long under blue summer skies.

And I just saw him recently, as I was strolling along the way;
I panicked – O my, he was among a crowd, I was afraid to go and afraid to stay,
An angry mob said they caught him shoplifting in broad daylight;
And they had beaten him up (to death) till the sun set to give the night.
Alas drug addict, smell did he not of marijuana when he eventually died,
Because he hadn't money to buy any and stealing was what he tried.

Choene Semenya

Ramblingly: awkwardly; **reek**: a bad smell; **Nyaope**: (from South Africa) a type of street drug containing a cocktail of ingredients like heroin, cannabis, and efavirenz; **commingling**: confusing, consisting of many things; **feebled**: made weak; **parched**: very thirst

GEOGRAPHY

Contours of her smile shaping the location of where my fate will end,
Running like rivers to find her flow stirred my chest like cyclones.
Past were her palm lines leading me to let bygones be.
Her body movement picked up a steady pace of the chameleon
that shed its colours to birth rainbows.
Her joy, that's where the rain goes,
Silver linings her encryptions coded in gathering cumulus,
Her wrists decked in shining bracelets of light mimicking thunder strikes.

She defines the red of my veins like, heat defining volcano jaws,
Oceans the only serenity where her mantras rises at
every wave gathering story to the shores,
Sands of time build good mementoes to discard pain through her pores.
She cut shapes of her beatific smile to particles of air,
Everytime I draw inscapes, she leaves a fresh breath of dawn on my face.

Atlas discarded the planet of his shoulders to see my world
shattered pieces of landscapes, where she taught time to sun,
whilst setting all movements of shadows off their shapes.
She knows where to find me even if I'm lost in translation.

Tshediso Seroki

HAVE MISSED MY SLEEP

How many days i don't KNOW!
a lotsa tossing and turning – sleepless nights,
owing to worries and sorrows about my plights;
Beneath a swift drift of moon and SNOW.

It was personal stress so bold i couldn't SHAKE,
took from me the energy from which the sleep is made;
my heart grieved, stained with agony that was hard to fade –
a heavy load to my shoulders, a burden i could no more TAKE.

The night, a time for sleep; for me a space to count my TEARS –
have missed my sleep counting my worries,
blaming myself and my puerile actions in series;
my wishes wasted unnecessarily on futile FEARS.

O dear, no more dreams and visions i could SEE
when at night i just tossed and turned –
till the light vanished and returned;
Oh the hopelessness, what on earth was happening to ME?

Choene Semenya

Puerile: childish, babyish; **futile**: pointless, senseless

HEAT

Chemistry to balance the heat composed to feelings decomposed
into memory of missing hits; love a contact sport where hearts bleed to
learn.
Son burns to turn into ashes of fading heat,
Heroes never wear Phoenix feathers to fly closer to the sun rays.
Well, curiosity pays, experience ask Icarus.
Heat hits the skin to bury flesh; bones keep getting exposed to warrior's
path.

Shades of heat creating mirage –
Shadows dance to the, what looks like water.
Thirst quenched from dry sands of burnt out memory;
Love lives under our chests like skeletons in closets.
Light and tunnels weird channels to find heat playing hide and seek
to seek where warmth resides.

Tshediso Seroki

Icarus: (the Latin spelling, conventionally adopted in English) is the son
of the master craftsman Daedalus, the creator of the Labyrinth

LAMENT FOR GRANDMA

Dear Grandma
In memory of you my eyes sadly well up with tears,
As I grieve, I can hardly breathe and can hardly think –
Now that your breath has fled your body; one of my fears
Of all times in life: to lose you, to see your body sink

Slowly, slowly, and slowly away from family and me.
Mind you I could not bear you suffer old age pain
But I always prayed that you lived longer than a Baobab tree;
And yet you passed on, hence I shall never see you again.

Age within you crept a little more with every passing day,
And withered thereof the lenses and the retina of your eyes;
It but with every step of ingress faded your hair gray,
Gave you nothing more than adversities in your speech and your sighs.

O, Gogo, with each break of dawn you advanced in years to grow old;
But as if I never knew that one day it was gonna be like this in the end
I could not stop wishing that your old age could disappear with the passing cold –
And I could see it in your eyes that you wished that it was but your intend.

O, God, the Father, I hardly ask anything from You throughout day and night,
So methinks amiss or too much would it not be for me to ask dearly from You
That You bequeath me daring to face the odds of day and the weight of plight;
I simply request You, to solace my family and bless my grandmother too.
Au revoir Grandma, and fare thee well for the best!

Choene Semenya

Intend: choice; **solace**: heal, comfort; **amiss**: wrong; **au revoir**: goodbye

VOODOO

Dolls, Ancient drums, Magic carpets —
Wrinkles of time unfold mysteries to new age.
Full moon takes form of crystal ball future is apartment on skyscraper;
Clouds for burning incense, summoning on an instant,
Investigation of a death of an infant.
Bones attached to strings, dolls obey spells to evoke dead spirits.

Souls bare-footed to tread sacred grounds, calabashes holding charms;
Wrinkled palms shake arms as music savour the moment of sacrifice.
White of eyes exposed to truth, the sky is a birthplace for stars.
Water speaks from opened scars.
Songs building moment until the body dies from flesh to live as spirits...
Another gentle palm print on the drum life is seen
And infant is found lying in ancestral basket where life is restored.

Tshediso Seroki

WHAT I SO MUCH HATE

In life
   I hate to be in the jolly memories of those
      whom I infatuated against whom which I loved,
To love so nearly and dearly those who always
   fail to love me back;
   I hate to seek for true love in vain of gain,
And to undergo the same tiresome process over and
   over again.
I hate to fail to give solace to those who in sooth
   need one from me,
To kiss my beloved ones in the glare of the limelight;
   I hate to trust implicitly those who tend to take
   advantage of me,
To jealous back those who unreservedly jealous me –
   I hate to write what I don't like,
To write what I think against what I truly feel.
   I hate to love conditionless those who love me conditionful,
To discriminate against people owing to the colour of their skin
   Or their ranks;
I hate to pretend to admire those whose sight boil my blood –
   To divulge secrets of those who confess in me
   with utmost confidence;
   And to be friends with someone who never listens to me.
I hate to count my tears and my curses against
   my joy and my blessings,
To count every day of the week and not
   make every day of the week count –
And, above all, so much hate do I
   To rely on myself and not on God.

Choene Semenya

Infatuated: besotted, smitten; **divulge**: reveal

THE EARTH

Lines on the loss of life

I

Lissome is the Earth with verges that are coarse and bold;
In solitude of life of this sanctimonious planet,
Our deep-rooted wishes wander all in vain.

II

In this planet of everlasting penury,
The parched turpitude of its cruelty overshadows
And shatters our dearest hopes to slake its thirst;

III

Even when the sun of our land endeavors to devour our worries away
And fade them forever;
The pedantic ego of the Earth vanquishes it with its perpetuated wrath
That conquers it with its overweening bumptiousness.

IV

Waking up in the midst of the night; gazing upon the orbs that
Shine to give us comfort – hoping to be solaced
But the gluttonous Earth quaffs them all with its unstoppable greed
And we again, left in pain.

V

In a breath of wind that attempts to blow and diminish our laments
Trees and the vanquished try to breathe to revive themselves;
But its unbidden void inhales all the fresh air available;

VI

Something there is that doesn't love our vim that tosses about this Earth;
Listening to its ventriloquistic loquacity that overwhelms the monologue
Of our threnodies about it,
'tis the Earth itself that flings an ocean of
rebukes at our presence upon it.

VII

The Earth hasn't a friend
Nor does it care for one's ambitions of life
Nor shall it ever lose possession of the greed it owns
Nor can it ever be able to distinguish 'twixt life and death
And seeking its mercy is much of a muchness looking for
A lost needle in a haystack
And us, we sink right DOWN!

Choene Semenya

Lissome: slim, not big; **solitude**: loneliness; **sanctimonious**: behaving as if you are more moral than others; **penury**: great poverty; **turpitude**: wickedness; **pedantic**: too worried about small details; **perpetuated**: made to last longer; **overweening**: showing too much confidence or pride; arrogant; **bumptiousness**: showing you think you are more important than others; **gluttonous**: greedy; **void**: a large empty space; **ventriloquistic:** the art of speaking without moving your lips and making it seem as if voice is coming from another person ; **loquacity**: talkativeness; **monologue**: a long speech spoken by one person, especially when alone; **threnodies**: laments; bemoans; regrets

THE NIGHT I KISSED HER LIPS

The night I kissed her lips was last May;
But the wind came and blew it all away:
Again I kissed her lips and made her weep,
But came the moon, and made my kiss her sleep.
'O what a man,' she exclaimed, 'that dost kiss me
With a kiss so mortal it could immortalised be –
But I myself shall say: I sincerely love this man,
And also his golden kiss, pleasant since it began;
Yet so, for this my love shall be eternised –
I shall solely love him, no trait compromised.'
O this wench, if lips were slain I'd slain hers last,
And nevermore shall I then kiss any lips or blast;
I shall let my lips die from penance and pride
For those lips that I kissed, were the best I ever eyed.

Choene Semenya

Wench: lady; **penance**: self-punishment; **blast**: party

SUITCASE

Memories full of quests unfulfilled, the more the merrier common prose.
When scars itch wounded soul path is heavy.
Diaries filled with tears as mind looks back but heart goes forth.
Bible for guide, watch to look out on new memories made.
A mirror to look for inner beauty,
A comb to find syllables underneath an itching sculp.
Photo frame to keep on the walls of broken hearts,
Brother, your luggage is full of skeletons like bone collector,
Yet your heart as hefty, carrying weight like balancing guilt on empty promises.
Sister, you keep changing faces like pavement ghost,
The shadow you have become has turned your womb into graveyard
where men and fetuses have learnt to die.
Layers keep piling up like sand granules through the hour glass,
This heavy casket is heavy to carry body
Walking to wake up to Death.

Tshediso Seroki

A LETTER TO A WEBSTER

Dear Webster:

They take delight in that they see you smile,
Because they hardly saw you joyous in a little while;
Quivering, cold and scared you looked to them ev'ryday.

You wallowed in misery, for ages mopping for yourself,
You took all kinds of anti-anxiety pills per day,
But none were there for your lament on the shelf.

Good friends, the whole time by, worrying about your state
Of sadness that made their hearts laden with hate,
Hate, hate against the deterioration of your health.

Good friends who popped by and sang your favourate songs,
And sorrowed, and cried as they wished you wellbeing and wealth,
Do not forget the days and times when you always counted your wrongs.

Good friends, how humble, whose hearts are yet full of delight,
Their eyes could blaze with merriment now at your contented sight
Somehow, taking deserved credit in that you rejoice again.

Because in every prayer, they evermore but prayed that you be gay,
Against curses, against fears, against tears and formidable pain,
Hence, worry no more of the past and think of the future, starting today.

Choene Semenya

THAT PAIN

Stars are known to the universe by names.
The wounds of your past still tattooed in your veins.

YES!

Family trees keep losing branches.
Young seeds trying to fit in roots,
that don't belong to their stem.
That pain doesn't belong to that soul;
those tears let them fall on their own.
Your heart has been broken,
more than once, more than twice.

Spiritual inclined women know the thin line
between submission and oppression.
Carve your pain into heavenly paint
to decorate your gushing scars;
Still it's the purpose of that pain that buried
dreams in our cold hearts.

Our chests are waste lands, no love grows there.
You see your neighbours eating almost nothing from table of poverty,
Mouths dry from praying – that pain is on the knees that pray,
To that street child Christmas comes as for of bread and milk.

Perhaps they have different version of Santa,
maybe their clause is Santa is not real.
That pain beneath your feet
doesn't belong to the step yet you about to take,
Those silent tears lament intent unattended.
That pain in the empty stomach
Resembles prayers of a commoner in discarded temple.

Maybe this poem, may not get rid of the pain
or take away your sad memory.
A poet may say plenty about his experience,
maybe or perhaps that pain is my poem.
Let that tongue to rip curls of uncoiling songs,
Sing for your organ, compose tunes from broken notes,
As beautiful music hails from there.

Tshediso Seroki

IN HER LIFE

Of all the sorrows that so govern her generous heart,
Her love is the most unfair thing breaks her apart;
In her life everything is already signed and sealed –
And she evermore solemnly griefs her soul appealed
To cheat, to relinquish, or to commit suicide and die
The death that shall liberate her of her perpetual cry.
Has providence deserted her, so unkindly in all facets of life
That she so feels old, unhappy and like a desperate housewife?
For alone she weeps, breathless with melancholy; her pouring tears
Desolate with bitterness, anger and incessant grief of discovered fears.
Her heart is weak, her soul is weaker –her love life is a scornful jest;
No endless joy, or liberty of love(a nice poor little girl by love depressed.)
   'Tis hard to dissever when love & pity have been merged in dim,
     When all that she wants is to love and to be fairly loved by him.

Choene Semenya

Appealed: tempted; **solemnly**: sadly; **relinquish**: give up; **perpetual**:
everlasting; **providence**: fate, destiny; **melancholy**: sadness; **desolate**:
deserted, forsaken; **incessant**: continuous; **dissever**: separate, apart from
something

CRY NOT BLACK MADONNA

Lessons learnt in up sense are discarded down here.
Inner sense a spectacle when man pursues fame and glamour;
Sons broke shields around their innocence, it hurts a mother more.
When paying mourning to a jail bird,
Broken heart still carry the what used to be frame –
When love is out of focus.

Madonna, mother, the black of your veil mourn the death of stars
that never made it to the cosmos;
I see your tears as twinkles that hope for rebirth of lost daughters.
Martyrs of events still haunted by spirits of elders
whose tears rusted chains under decks of MERCHANT ships;
The rust of shackles around your smile resembles a sad face.

I have seen how many times you pray for sons and daughters
fighting war against addiction and drug abuse.
I have heard your pleas at every dying day that night spares
the life of your only son – sirens summon fears;
Your nights are stained with sleepless tears.
I know you pray for their wellbeing,
Your palm prints doesn't want to part ways with your rosary,
for it hears your lips miming words like eventually prayer pays.

Mother of nation as black as silence,
Time is a bandage that wraps wounds to hide the scars away.
In your prayers' breath, tongue picks dust like unused library,
spiritual pockets full of tears, knees dented,
Exhalation marvel upon mystery of life.

Madonna cry not, for morning comes with hope.

Tshediso Seroki

ZIMBABWEAN CRIPPLED BEGGAR

Sprawling was he in the roasting sun outside an Indian store.
Shaking and jingling coins in his begging bowl hoping to receive more;
Just as his hunger grew terrible in his begging tummy,
Some rich man gave him a tit-bit of pizza, it tasted richly yummy.
Though the reek of his shoes was yay stuffy, his raiment soberly tattered –
And his body smelt malodorous but none of that to him ever mattered.
He'd grin wide his pitch yellow teeth and germ-favoured gums,
opening his creased hands seeking alms;
And he'd do it over and over and over again, with sweat tumbling
from 'twixt his crying palms.
He'd sing lamentable songs of elegy, with grime of perspiration and muck
on his face;
Weeping solemnly to everyone that passed by the town's market place –
Alas! His tears recalled where the coins had fled, the coins of pledge of
the piteous beggar;
His begging bowl full of coins was seized by a snatcher, a very heartless
drabber.
Oh poor crippled Zimbabwean Beggar, his weeping was all in vain,
Cos that rich man was probably never gonna feed him, again.

Choene Semenya

Sprawling: sitting awkwardly; **tit-bit**: a small piece of delicious food; **reek**: stench, unpleasant smell; **yay stuffy**: extremely stinky because of lack of fresh air; **his raiment soberly tattered**: his clothes seriously old and torn; **malodorous**: smelling unpleasant; **germ-favoured**: full of germs; **creased**: wrinkled; **alms**: money or food that are given to poor people; **'twixt**: between; **elegy**: a sad poem or song about a dead person; **solemnly**: seriously

THE HOURGLASS BROKE

We keep searching for a soul.
We try to find light in times of darkness,
Trying so hard never to let go.

It's for you to lift your head up, shoulders in shape of a guitar,
every embrace music to live for.
Firmament a place where slaves of hardships find light,
Heart fights with beating to escape the chest,
Our skeletons on the hunt for flesh to cover their nakedness;

Truth is,
Nobody wants to die to become an angel,
But amazingly everyone wants to go to heaven.
Our minds plotting wishful thinking every so oft,

Eyes with continuous blinking –
Look! The beauty lies naked and pure.

In this time we search for limits in times of our sorrow.
We keep faith glued to our sight;
Nobody wants to hold darkness for a light.
In between your wars, your body wants to faint with reason,
if this happens don't give In.

The search is on every night when shadows on revolt,
Art of living is not coded with expectations, yet live
In faint belief that the storm will pass loss at
Your scars for they shine at night.

In presence of your demons swallow your pride,
let your screams turn into a roar,
For now your enemies know you declared war.
The war between colour and race blind the seeking eye.
Behold your brother's keep; comfort his broken heart in times of weep.

The bond of love is deep – have you followed your heart or
has your heart followed you to where you heading?

When Hourglass glass breaks, it's our inner peace that seeks refuge,
Sand disappear within our cracked skins.
Memory dances like a temperamental cyclone for we keep
twisting our spines to grab attention of those who don't value us.
Child, God will use your voice for a greater good,
don't let a mere mortal stand in front of your greatness.
Believe!!!!

Tshediso Seroki

THE PRINCIPAL AND HIS CABLE

The grumpy principal athwart the class
is walloping the learner ad infinitum
with his computer cable,
and screeching his lungs out
his wrath and his tranquilities;
he says she's late for school yet again.

Madly she pulls across the desks;
pleads for pity in pigsty floors,
whilst he despite his heavy paunch
chases and corners her.

He whips and whips the weeping non-plussed
girl till the cable slips in his hand. Her tears are
like explosion of waterfall in her cheeks and her pain
still so fresh·

He picks it up and pursues the poor girl
who endeavours to escape from him. She
jumps and climbs atop the desks on her way
to the classroom door but quickly plummets to
the floor to receiving another angry wallop.

As hard as he can he strikes the poor girl till his
hairless bald is dripping wet with sweat. The
learner's heart is a watershed of fear words
can't even describe. His visage is sadistic and
turns into something I never liked or loved…

Well, it is over now and the poor girl is
sobbing sadly in the library,
Yet the principal plunges and slouches
over his circling chair in his office. His lips mumbling,

pooped out –In slight remorse of the cruel hiding
he'd given the poor learner; and lugubriously he envisions
the twinge she's had to bear, but it ain't no use
for what's done is done.

Choene Semenya

Walloping: whip; **ad infinitum**: over and over again; **screeching**:
screaming; **tranquilities**: goodness and calmness; **pigsty**: dirty; **paunch**:
a big stomach of a man; **non-plussed**: confused; **endeavours**: tries; **atop**:
on top of; **plummets**: falls heavily; **dripping wet**: extremely wet; **sadistic**:
seeming to get pleasure from hurting others; **slouches**: sits awkwardly;
pooped out: completely tired; **remorse**: regret; **lugubriously**: sadly;
envisions: imagines; **twinge**: pain

WILLIAM SHAKESPEARE IS MY FAVOURATE POET

William Shakespeare is my favourate poet!

It does not need a thousand poems, dear,
to prove that William Shakespeare
is a scintillating poet, nor does it require
him to write so many sonnets or tire

His ambidextrous pen and his gifted wrist
writing romantic ballads with a twist
in the end – his poems vivifies the air,
especially when his poetry is about despair.

William Shakespeare is my favourate poet of all days;
I like how he writes, his styles and his ways;
his poems written with words embellished,
with his thoughts and his ideas dearly wished –

His imagery is pure, his emotions are raw,
a tale of poems that always make my day so braw;
as fair enough twice the generosity of the sea,
Sterling I say, to make him my favourate poet be;

From how he wrote 'Shall I compare thee. . .'
To how he structured his poem 'Soliloquy',
And won people's hearts with 'Let me not to the marriage of True minds',
When he said, and I quote: 'Which alters when alteration finds,

Or bends with the remover to remove. Oh no!'
William Shakespeare, this poet was such a pro –
He owed the world definitions of his words of charm,
which always but so puzzled the mind though meant no harm.

His antique English inspired and fascinated me to read his work,
His sonnets, full of metaphors and similes that evermore but had his back –
Tell you what, no poet can write close to how Shakespeare ever wrote,
For the master of poetry ever lived and died, and vanished with a quote.

That is, inter alia, why William Shakespeare is my favourite poet!

Choene Semenya

Scintillating: brilliant, entertaining; **ambidextrous**: equally skillful with each hand; **embellished**: decorated; **braw**: from Scottish meaning fine; **sterling**: excellent; **soliloquy**: monologue, speech one makes to themselves; **antique**: old, ancient

A TRUE HERO HAS DEPARTED

Tribute to Tata Madiba

Nelson Rolihlahla Mandela, Madiba *1918 -2013*

O Tata Nelson Rolihlahla Madiba Mandela, our dear,
The son of the African soil, our most audacious leader –
'Tis sorrowful to know you've finally breathed your last,
You, a genuine global icon with a wonderfully inspiring past;
'Twas quite pellucid that age had wasted you with ailments
And your sporadic illness perturbed us overmuch, but who repents
Now that you repose from your tribulations and your pain?
Even though it is sad that shall we never see you again.

As profound but your selflessness and courage constitute an enormous loss,
Though it is ideal that you fulfilled your promise to eradicate the gross.
There are so many deaths in process that the road to heaven must be convoy,
But your clairvoyance and your diligence shall see you through and bring you joy –
In wholeness, I am confident that your road and yours per se is the road of kings,
The road richly and abundantly blessed, the one censored by an angel who sings.
You may have departed, however, it would take more than just death to perish you –
Nothing close to something will fill your gap; you'll be in heaven and with us too,

In spirit of course; nothing at all shall batter your legendary state,
You, a true hero who is incapable of vengeance and hate.
A humble African warrior who lived and loved without pride,
One giant martyr of apartheid who lived with nothing to hide;
We cherish and honour your legacy, You, the greatest leader of the 21st century,

If I could I would but take all the words and time in the world to write your obituary.
We mourn your death, His Excellency, and we celebrate but your majestic life;
We lament together with your widow, Mam' Graça Machele, your beautiful wife.

You are the fairest man I know, whose heart knows no evil and no disarray,
You're near and dear to our hearts and never shall we forget you when we pray,
You the man who boldly cultured peace and put oppression of one by another to the end –
O Tata Madiba, we bid you adieu, bon voyage on your celestial departure, our beloved friend.
You've truly achieved a surplus of what can be expected of man,
You've set an indelible mark from the day your detention began;
When you were sent and sequestered to Robben Island, a place of banishment,
Where you were persecuted for having faith in vision for betterment.

You endured a litany of torturous unspeakable acts without (choice) scope,
But never had you glanced to your hind or abandoned freedom as your hope –
Detained and plagued for being a good man, 27 years were you in jail
And you remained as good as good could be when were you denied bail.
Then 11 February 1990, you officially returned home – your heart devoid of bitterness,
Your soul peaceably at ease as you'd trodden the streets of Soweto in total happiness

Aah Dhalibunga!
We salute you Nelson, for your sacrifices, humanity and desire for unity right through,
But most of all, for not acting vengeful towards those who inflicted pain unto you.
Oh I hail you a true hero, Dalibhunga, and if there's anything from you I'd learnt,
Is but for the truce and but for a fair life's sake, what peace and reconciliation meant –

You taught me to be true to myself, to speak my thoughts and to render peace;

You rescued black nation from oppression and injustice and had put their life at ease.

We extend our indebtedness to the magnitude of your greatness and your prominence,

As we stand to behold the outcome of your industrious democratic effort and excellence.

Your Royal Highness, may it be that your pilgrimage is majestic and dignified;

The joy and all the peace you shall get in the afterlife, may they too be glorified –

Nothing will sum up just what a great man you are, not even a book extended

to a thousand mile;

Dear Rolihlahla, those were my final words to you as I bid you farewell and bid you farewell awhile.

Thank you ever so much indeed Tata Madiba! Rest in Peace!

Praise Dalibhunga, praise.

Choene Semenya

Audacious: brave; **clairvoyance**: having psychic powers; **disarray**: chaos; **bon voyage on your celestial departure**: goodbye on your heavenly trip; **plagued**: punished; **prominence**: state of importance

PARDON ME MY LORD

From a remorseful Zionist

O dear Lord, it is impossible for one to be flawless in any way,
Even for those who go to church every Sunday;
I know I wronged You my Lord; I defied You –
I've gone against Your will and cohabited with those wearing blue.

I used to discompose others; to rob and maraud and steal,
But I guess now I know how those I robbed feel;
Let all those stolen belongings and goods I sold,
My Lord, not haunt me 'til I grow old.

I know I had a cast-iron habit to kill –
I would sneak and scheme and plot until
I had my victims, Your children my Lord,
Under a spell of death; I throttled them with a cord.

I slept with other men's wives –
And I survived sharp blades of knives;
My friends say I'm valiant regarding what I learnt,
If only I even knew what that meant.

I know, my Dearest Lord, I deserve a punishment of a life;
Pardon me, for never can I repose in the midst of this colossal strife.
And please, whisper the truth into my ears,
And see if I have an ear that hears.

Help me away my sins and right my wrongs,
Teach me Your praises and Your songs;
And give me another chance to build a name
That I shall pride myself with, for Christianity and not for fame.

To groom me and to learn to trust me again,
Despite this people who treat me with disdain.
O Holy Spirit, dismiss thou this contempt flickering within me,
And humour me with a charismatic self that I can forever be.

Choene Semenya

Flawless: perfect; **defied**: disobeyed, disrespected; **cohabited**: lived with women without marrying them; **discompose**: intimidate, threaten; **maraud**: going from place to place looking for people to kill, rob and so on; **cast-iron**: unbreakable; **valiant**: very brave; **colossal strife**: heavy and strong bitterness; **contempt**: tendency of not having fears, worries and so on; **charismatic**: that worships God in an enthusiastic way

PART II

AUTHORS' MUSE

THRENODY OF A DROWNED FUTURE

All hopes have been shattered,
All beliefs torn asunder,
All souls tormented,
All ambitions crushed to smithereens,
All dreams sank deep down a villainous drain;
Wishes and desires vanished plumb into thin air:
O my, Lord O dear, all gone like mist before the sun.

Choene Semenya

Threnody: a lament; bemoan; **asunder**: apart; **smithereens**: smaller fragments; **villainous:** wicked; very unpleasant

THE WAITRESS

Tardily with smarmy smiles and flaxen hair
After longest endless shifts of night and day how unfair
She appears from the restaurant's kitchen door
And tiredly limps to help he who airily waves at her down the floor
To order dinner's preprandial, the one he will enjoy
The oke who wants to order, his name is Elroy.

Choene Semenya

Tardily: slowly; **smarmy**: too polite in a way that's not sincere; **flaxen**: pale yellow; blonde; **limps**: walks awkwardly with difficulty; **preprandial**: happening immediately before a main meal; **oke**: from South African meaning man

ART OF BROKEN MEN

After consecutive blows on his ego, he became a broken man and broken men break everything even if they try to fix it. He lost his job over the argument with a manager; his frustrations led him to the shebeen. There he drank all his frowns for a premature smile that he saw on the dance floor. What's more to lose if not the remaining dented pride? Then reality suddenly knocked on his drunken stupor. He paused, he looked at the watch it gazed him back in the eye with such piercing silence. He remembered himself on the household left without a father figure. He drank from broken hourglass where his mouth tasted bitter reality crystals for crystal. He walked out of the shebeen with liquefied demons screaming from his right hand. He wants to be whole again – yet he breaks his heart more.

Tshediso Seroki

BLEEDING

Her heart keeps bleeding, you strike a woman you strike a rock placed on a test; She wears shades of happiness – no, her smiled attached to emptiness.

Her womb put to the test, her wounded spine carrying more, she knows no rest.
In case she was fighting, her knees became useless to prayers made out of deflated lungs; she cries more for her daughters and sons . . .
She still smiles though.

Tshediso Seroki

THE QUESTION

There is this liquid voice
I hear piercing the air,
Through the ears –
Across the clods of hearts;
Gobbling the damp tedium
of noiseless quietude of
the stillest hours of night
and day: it is over and again
the dulcet voice of that bard
rendering yet her rhyming poem
full of rhyming rhymes.

Also, there is this perilous poacher
I used to see, exploiting nature,
Through the forest of nature reserves –
Across the shrank creaking trees of Kruger National Park;
Poaching rhinos for their superstitiously
priceless horns, rather unceremoniously;
Rhinos of the lively conservational scenery night
and day: it is now him, the perilous poacher,
I see, poached by rangers
full of raging rage.

And if, too, this serial murderer
Shall with his mortal self, escape,
Through the angry mob –
Across the wrath of pangas
and guns and swords and knives
and stones and steel wires and axes
without taste of mob justice like that night
in this very day: then it is definitely maybe
that this mob ain't wanna murder him
for their hearts are
full of forgiving forgiveness.

Then it is a question now:
Whether 'tis nobler
To listen to the rhyming rhymes
Or look at the poacher poached
Or watch the murderer murdered.

Liquid: clear, pure and flowing; **dulcet**: sounding sweet and pleasant; **perilous**: dangerous; **unceremoniously**: without caring about their feelings; **mortal**: living; **Kruger National park**: in northeastern South Africa, is one of Africa's largest game reserves.

LIMERICK (PIE ENTHUSIAST)

Suddenly my pal collapsed and faced at the sky,
I heard his kid sisters shriek a painful cry.
Though from town, his mother came with an appetizing pie,
And my pal lickety-split woke up; we knew he did not die.
Know you why he woke up: for he smelt the pie pass by.

Choene Semenya

Lickety-split: immediately; very quickly

FINNY-FUNNY LIMERICK

He was like his brother, Jacob;
He was lazy and he had no job.
He lived without a house, family and a wife,
He was so demotivated that he wasted his life –
Each day he'd mop himself, and weep and sob!

Choene Semenya

Adamant: stubborn; **sobriety**: drunken state; **sans**: without

I AM BLACK

I am black!
Look!
Look at the hue of my skin – 'tis black!
I am black at nightfall;
I am black in the morn and during the noonday:
And even if rough winds
And hardships batter me –
I'll still be beauteous,
Cos I am unapologetically black!

Choene Semenya

Nightfall: dusk; the time of the day when it gets dark; **batter**: damage

STRANGER

There was once a tall dark stranger,
Who traveled in a white ford ranger –
He was odd and he was fraught with anger;
He was paedophilic and to kids he was pure danger!

Choene Semenya

Paedophilic: tending to be sexually attracted to children

About The Poets

Semenya, Choene Alley (1992 –)

Choene Alley Semenya is a South African born proficient English author and intellectual poetry writer hailing from the small village of Moletjie Ga-Matamanyane in Limpopo province. He is a pharmacist by profession, and also serves as an academic lecturer at Sefako Makgatho Health Sciences University (SMU) where he has currently enrolled for his Masters of Pharmacy (M.Pharm) specializing in Pharmaceutical Chemistry, in Pretoria, South Africa. Mr. Semenya defines poetry as a platform to tell the truth, to impart knowledge and experiences through valuable writing for fun and leisure. Whilst in his childhood he was bedazzled by, and excelled in literature. Much of his work is focused on fantasy and romantic fiction, and is mostly dedicated to newly literate adults.

Seroki, Tshediso (1984 –)

Tshediso Seroki, real name Tshediso Andries Louw, is a very flexible poet and a motivational speaker who hails from a small town named Kroonstad in The Free State, South Africa. He is the eldest of his siblings and his parents are oblivious that he is writer. Growing up, ideally Tshediso was very fond of becoming a Medical Doctor; however, after obtaining his National Diploma in Diagnostic Radiography(N. DIP RADIOGRAPHY DIAGNOSTIC) from the Central University of Technology he now practices as Diagnostic Radiographer at Tokollo Hospital located in Heilbron in the Free State. He has started since performing on open-mic sessions from 2013 and is still trying to find his voice on stage. He is a passionate lover of words and he is quite hungry for excellence.

Printed in the United States
By Bookmasters